FOUNDERS
OF GREAT RELIGIONS

FOUNDERS
OF GREAT RELIGIONS

BEING PERSONAL SKETCHES OF FAMOUS
LEADERS

By

MILLAR BURROWS, Ph.D.

ASSOCIATE PROFESSOR OF BIBLICAL LITERATURE AND HISTORY OF
RELIGIONS IN BROWN UNIVERSITY

CHARLES SCRIBNER'S SONS, NEW YORK

CHARLES SCRIBNER'S SONS, Ltd., LONDON

1935

PREFACE

In offering an introduction to some of the principal living religions through biographical sketches of their founders I am not unmindful of the fact that every religion is the product of a social movement. The life of each great leader, in religion as in other enterprises, is largely determined by the conditions of his own particular age and land, and his contribution is but one of many interwoven strands in a fabric that is always changing. This little book, however, does not attempt to unravel that complicated texture. As a matter of fact, valuable as it would be to place each founder's life in a definite social setting and analyze the factors which determined it, we do not know enough to do this. If we try to do it, with the facts at our disposal, we must supplement them with so much speculation that the result can hardly be described as history. All that the present work attempts, therefore, is to tell the story as it has come down through the centuries, with sufficient selection and explanation to produce a fairly consistent account. Only in a few instances have I suggested hypotheses of my own. Speculative theories, even when offered by scholars of repute, have been for the most part ignored.

If little effort is made to supply what our sources do not tell, neither is the sifting of true from false in the stories themselves undertaken in any thorough-going fashion. Occasional indications of greater or less probability are given, but the purpose of the book does not involve the elimination of every unhistorical element in the traditions. There may be more real value — both religious and historical — in a legend than in a modern scholar's reconstruction of events and circumstances. A legend often reflects faithfully the real character of its hero. Even if the personality represented by tradition is unhistorical, it is the personality actually venerated by the adherents of the religion and expresses their ideals and aspirations. To understand the religion one must know the picture of the founder given by the accepted traditions. This point of view, which will be found expressed in the introduction, is not maintained with equal consistency in all the following chapters, but the book as a whole is governed by it and should be so understood.

In the desire to produce at a low price a book of interest to the general public, "documentation"—the darling of a scholar's heart—has been omitted. For the same reason the index and bibliography have been made very brief. Some indication, therefore, should be given here as to the authorities for the materials and views presented. As far as I could, I have gone directly to primary sources. In the Old and New Testaments, and to a lesser degree in the Koran, I was able to use the original languages. For the other sacred writings I was dependent upon translations; whenever possible, however, different versions have been compared. Of course my interpretation of these sources has been affected, to an extent I cannot measure or define, by the views expressed in standard works on the history of religions in general and on the founders in particular — works which I have had constant occasion to use as a teacher of the history of religions. Where I am conscious of dependence on a particular writer, the fact is indicated in the text.

My principal authorities, however, are the scriptures themselves.

Except in the chapters on Moses, Nanak, and Jesus, most
of the direct quotations are taken, with only a few slight
alterations, from the *Sacred Books of the East*. In the chapter on Mahavira a few passages are quoted also from Mrs.
Sinclair Stevenson's *Heart of Jainism*. The quotations in
the chapter on Nanak are from M. A. Macauliffe's *The
Sikh Religion: Its Gurus, Sacred Writings and Authors*.
For permission to quote from these works I am indebted to
the Clarendon Press of Oxford. Some of the material quoted
in the chapter on Lao-tze is taken from *The Canon of
Reason and Virtue*, a translation of the Tao-Teh-King by
Paul Carus, and some of the quotations in the chapter on
Buddha are from the same writer's *Gospel of Buddha*, a
selection from the Buddhist scriptures. Permission to quote
from these two books has been kindly granted by the Open
Court Publishing Company. The introductory chapter contains a paragraph from Edmond Fleg's *Life of Moses*, used
by permission of E. P. Dutton and Company, and many
stories in the chapter on Moses are derived from the same
book. Quotations from the Bible do not regularly follow any
one version.

In the spelling of names the forms adopted are those
which seem to be most common in English. To be consistent
one should write *Laocius* if he writes *Confucius,* or *Kung-
fu-tze* if he writes *Lao-tze*. Some of our English forms of
the names, moreover, are poor transliterations of the origi-
nals. For the general reader, however, unfamiliar spelling
would only produce confusion.

To Professor Henry T. Fowler of Brown University, who

read my work in manuscript and made several suggestions
for its improvement, I wish to express my appreciation. In
the collection and selection of materials invaluable assistance
was given by my wife, to whom the book is gratefully dedi-
cated.

MILLAR BURROWS.

BEIRUT, SYRIA,
   January 1, 1931.

CONTENTS

FOUNDERS OF GREAT RELIGIONS

CHAPTER ONE

INTRODUCTION

THE importance of knowing something about other religions than our own is coming to be generally recognized. Just as one does not really know his own language until he has some knowledge of other languages, so an acquaintance with other religions is necessary for a true understanding of our own. Not for this reason only, but also for the sake of understanding the people of other lands, a knowledge of their religions is important. Modern transportation and communication have multiplied our contacts with other nations and races, making it more and more imperative that we should try to understand their ways of thinking and living. Nothing is more essential to this end than a knowledge of the religion in which each people's basic ideals and convictions are expressed. Religion is one of the dominant forces in human life. Neither the individual nor the social group is truly known so long as religion is left out of account. To know fully either ourselves or our neighbors, therefore, we must know something of the world's religions.

No better beginning can be made toward the understanding of a religion than a study of its founder's life and teaching. In approaching any subject nowadays we use the historical method: we ask not simply what a thing is, but how it came to be so. Religions, like all living and growing things, are complicated affairs, not easily comprehended in a brief and simple description. Take, for example, our own religion. We speak of Christianity as one religion, as though it were a single and definite system of beliefs and practices. But what is Christianity? Is it Protestantism or Catholicism, Modernism or Fundamentalism? When we claim that Christianity is the best and highest of the world's religions, do we mean that everything which goes by the name of Christianity is better than anything which goes by the name of Hinduism or Judaism? Does our claim of superiority include the Coptic and Nestorian Churches of the East along with the many varieties of American Protestantism? Someone has said that Christianity is not a religion but a family of religions; certainly it is anything but simple and homogeneous. And a similar diversity is found in all the great religions.

In the case of Christianity it is not unusual to seek the unity underlying this diversity by a return to the simple teaching of the founder. Many modern Christians hold that we must go back of all mediæval forms and doctrines and look to Jesus himself for the essential meaning of Christianity. Some even claim allegiance to the founder and reject the organized religion which is called by his name. In the Orient there are many earnest spirits who are willing to accept Christ but not Christianity. The recent missionary conference at Jerusalem declared that the gospel which the church has for the world is Christ himself. In the teaching of the founder we find the original form of the religion. Nothing could be more natural or more reasonable, therefore, than to look to the founder of each religion for its distinctive spirit, its essential genius.

To be sure, the study of the religions cannot stop with the founders. Their place in the religious history of mankind must not be exaggerated. No religion, we must always remember, is wholly the creation of any individual. We commonly distinguish the personally founded religions from those which evolved gradually out of earlier forms, like Hinduism in India and Shinto in Japan. But even the religions which most distinctly owe their origin to individuals have had a background in older beliefs and practices. No new religion has ever succeeded in shaking off entirely the influence of the faith from which it arose. In ancient Egypt a high-minded Pharaoh tried to break away from the past and his religion died with him. To a lesser degree Zoroaster tried it, but his teaching survived only through compromise and mixture with the older beliefs of the people. Sometimes new faiths first appear as reforms or revivals within older religions. Confucius did not even attempt to establish a new religion, and Jesus had no intention of doing so—his purpose was to fulfil the law and the prophets.

Not only are the men we call founders dependent upon the past, but they are also at the mercy of the future. A religion is the expression of a social movement; it bears the impress of many personalities, the impress of the life of a whole group through many generations. The diversity which we have noted in Christianity is no less characteristic of the other religions. In each of them there have been so many different movements and tendencies that a description of the religion which is simple is for that very reason inadequate and misleading.

Clearly the distinction between founders and reformers is only relative. The changes which have taken place in every religion have not always been for the worse, and the first great leader has not always been the most important. It is not easy to decide, for example, whether Moses should really be called the founder of Judaism, or whether it owes its genius more to the prophets of later centuries. Some historians have even argued that Paul was the real founder of Christianity as a religion separate from Judaism, and certainly Christianity would have been very different without him. The selection of certain individuals, therefore, as the founders of the religions, involves a rather arbitrary distinction.

This means, by the way, that the distinction between a religion and a sect is likewise only relative. Often the differences between two sects within a religion are as great as the differences between two religions. Liberal Protestantism and Liberal Judaism are not farther apart than liberal Protestantism and the Christianity of the Abyssinian Church. Protestantism itself might be called a new religion; indeed it has been affirmed that Modernism and Fundamentalism are two different religions. If we arrange the religions in a horizontal row and the sects within each religion in a vertical column, we may say that the horizontal distances between religions are no greater than the vertical distances between some of the sects.

All this is worth bearing in mind; for our present purpose, however, we may be content to accept the customary classification of religions and select our list of founders accordingly. While we realize that their experiences and teachings were rooted in the past, and that their religions have not remained as they left them, we shall find them none the less worth studying, and an acquaintance with them will give us at least the beginning of an understanding of the religions which they founded, without the confusing complexity and diversity which appear in the later forms of the religions.

Even the study of the founders is not such a simple matter as we might suppose. Certain difficulties must be recognized at the outset. To begin with, it is not easy to free ourselves from prejudice when we consider men whose ideas and ways are radically different from our own. But understanding and appreciation are impossible with prejudice. We must not allow ourselves to think of the founders of religions other than our own as queer old heathen. Loyalty to our own faith must not make us look for flaws in the other religions or in the lives and characters of their founders, nor must it blind us to their merits.

On the other hand, if we succeed in avoiding such an adverse attitude, we are in danger of falling over backwards into an uncritical enthusiasm, which after all is just another kind of prejudice. Sometimes people who have found more truth and value in other faiths than they expected are so carried away by the discovery that they unduly magnify the weaknesses of their own religion, or fail to see those of the one which has aroused their admiration. To say, for example, that the Koran is superior to the Bible, because it has both spiritual vision and poetic beauty, is to make a very hasty and superficial judgment. Such lack of balance in the appreciation of the ancient faiths of the Orient is by no means uncommon. To combine in due proportion the critical and the sympathetic attitude is one of the greatest difficulties of such a study as this.

Having achieved the right attitude, we must also secure reliable information, and this too is by no means easy. The field of study through which we must range for the facts we need is so vast that a first-hand knowledge of all of it is impossible. To learn all the languages in which the sources of our information are written would be the task of a life-time. We are dependent, therefore, upon specialists in each division of the field, and when they do not give us what we want, or when they disagree, we are quite helpless.

Even if we were not dependent upon translations and secondary sources, we should not have such information as we should like to have. Complete and trustworthy biogra-phies of the founders of the living religions are extremely scarce in any language. Most of our information comes from writings that are very old and have passed through a long process of transmission, often involving considerable alteration from time to time. Even so, in most cases, they do not go back to the times of which they tell. The stories they contain were often handed down by word of mouth for centuries before they were put into writing at all. Con-sequently history and legend are inextricably tangled to-gether. In two or three cases the records were composed not long after the founder's death, but even in these the legen-dary element is prominent. To know how far the stories which have come down to us embody historical fact, and how far they are the result merely of pious imagination, is frequently impossible. Occasionally we even find two in-compatible versions of the same story and have no means of telling which of them comes nearer to the truth.

Fortunately there are some compensations for these dif-ficulties. When we find a story full of supernatural elements, we need not regard it therefore as entirely unhistorical. An-cient peoples, like untutored folk in our own day, knew no such distinction as we draw between the natural and the supernatural. Whatever appeared to them extraordinary was inevitably reported in terms of what we call the miraculous. Stories of miraculous events must be critically weighed, of course, but they sometimes enshrine important facts of history. To eliminate the miracles of Jesus, for example, from the story of his life would certainly do violence to historical truth. However we may interpret them, they at least represent the fact, which no competent historian would deny, that Jesus was a healer as well as a preacher. We need not despise our sources because we find them teeming with supernatural events and beings.

More important than an exact account of what actually happened is an accurate picture of a historic personality. What Buddha did is not so essential for us as what he was. Fortunately a legend may present a true portrait of the person of whom it is told. Not every legend has even this degree of historicity, but when we find a more or less consistent picture of a definite personality shining through the legends told about a man, we may reasonably infer that the picture is essentially true to fact. And this is what we actually do find in the stories of all the founders of the world's religions. With regard to events we are often in the dark; with regard to the man himself we have, in the main, a fair degree of trustworthy knowledge, though not as much as we should like to have. Without attempting to discuss the many problems of authenticity and historicity, therefore, we may take the picture as it has come down to us and try to find in it the personality with which we wish to become acquainted.

Even if the founder's personality itself should prove to be in part or in whole legendary, it would still have a real historical importance. As a matter of fact, the founder in whom the adherents of a religion believe is the founder presented by the legends. Whether the stories are historical or not, they are accepted by the people, and the person they depict is the person venerated as the founder of the religion, even if the actual founder was quite a different man. As each religion has grown, its believers have so revered their founder that they have in imagination made him what they think he should have been. In so doing they have revealed their own ideals and attitudes. To understand the religion, therefore, it is as important to know the legendary figure as the historical person.

This is well illustrated by the following passage from the preface to Edmond Fleg's remarkable *Life of Moses:* "In the creative memory of Israel the Biblical Moses lives on, transfigured by a tradition rich in wonderful legends. Whilst *critical* exegesis, tracing back myths and rites to their supposed origins, would lead us to a primitive, savage Moses, wholly alien to our world of to-day, the religious, moral, poetical and satirical exegesis of our Rabbis has, with its symbols and its anachronisms, drawn the prophet nearer to us from century to century. Doubtless the real life of Moses will never be known *scientifically:* but is not this life, as Israel has imagined it, interpreted it, and felt it through the ages, also History? And is this history ended?"

With all these facts in mind we may now turn to the lives and teachings of the founders of humanity's great faiths, making what use we can of the materials at our disposal. In the following pages each founder will be discussed in turn, and a concluding chapter will attempt a general comparison of them all. The purpose of this comparison, however, will not be to determine which religion or which founder is the greatest. That question each reader must answer for himself. All that will be here attempted is to see just what there is in common between these great spiritual seers of different peoples, and what are the principal differences between them.

CHAPTER TWO

LAO-TZE

PHILOSOPHER AND MYSTIC

THE first founder we shall study is the one, it seems safe to say, of whom the least is known. Very little is told of his life, and not even that can be confidently accepted as historical, though in its main outlines it is not at all improbable. Lao-tze, the founder of Taoism, was a Chinese philosopher who lived in the days of the prophet Jeremiah. He was born, if we may accept the traditional date, in the year 604 B.C., not far from the time when western Asia witnessed the overthrow of the mighty Assyrian Empire by a Babylonian prince named Nebuchadnezzar, and about a hundred years before the establishment of democratic forms of government in Athens and Rome—young cities far away in the West of which Lao-tze never heard.

According to a native historian, when Lao-tze was born he was given a name meaning "Ear." After his death this was changed to one meaning "Long-eared," and it is supposed that this indicates a physical peculiarity. The name Lao-tze, by which the sage is usually known, is variously translated "Old Philosopher," "Old Gentleman," and "Old Boy." The last interpretation agrees with the legend that Lao-tze was carried in his mother's womb more than seventy years and was born with white hair, a story which seems to reflect the feeling of his contemporaries that the sage was a whole lifetime ahead of them in wisdom. Legge, the scholar to whom we owe the standard translation of most of the Chinese sacred books, suggests that the name probably originated from the fact that Confucius, who was about fifty years younger than Lao-tze, referred to the latter as "the Old Philosopher." The same Chinese characters may also be interpreted as meaning "Old Boy," and the legend presumably grew out of this misinterpretation.

We know nothing of Lao-tze's early life or training. Earlier writers seem to be quoted in the book which he wrote later in his life, and this may indicate that he was well educated. We know that he married, and his descendants were traced to the first century before our era. We can also be sure that he was renowned for his wisdom and had many followers. An interesting though somewhat puzzling glimpse into his private life is afforded by the following anecdote: Attracted by the fame of Lao-tze's wisdom a man came from a great distance to see him. Having seen and heard the sage, however, he was disappointed, nor did he hesitate to express his disappointment. "Now I perceive," said he, "that you are not a sage. Because there was some rice left about the holes of the rats, you sent away your younger sister, which was unkind; when your food, whether raw or cooked, remains before you not all consumed, you keep on hoarding it up to any extent." As the English translator says, these are strange charges to bring against the philosopher, and they make us wish that we knew more of Lao-tze's domestic life and personal history. But, the story continues, Lao-tze received his visitor's abuse with silence and an appearance of indifference.

The next day the visitor returned and said that his feelings had changed over night, and he could not tell what had brought about the change. To this Lao-tze responded simply by saying that he did not claim to be wise and would have shown no resentment if the man had called him an ox or a horse: "My manner was what I continually observe;—I did not put it on for the occasion." Thereupon the visitor "sidled away out of Lao-tze's shadow; then he retraced his steps, advanced forward, and asked how he should cultivate himself."

Now it was Lao-tze's turn to show that he could express the frankest criticism. "Your demeanor," he observed, "is repelling; you stare with your eyes; your forehead is broad and yet tapering; you bark and growl with your mouth; your appearance is severe and pretentious; you are like a horse held by its tether, you would move, but are restrained, and (if let go) would start off like an arrow from a bow; you examine all the minutiæ of a thing; your wisdom is artful, and yet you try to look at ease. All these are to be considered proofs of your want of sincerity. If on the borders one were to be found with them, he would be named a Thief." How charming is Oriental courtesy!

Apparently it was Lao-tze's custom to reprove his own disciples in this frank fashion. On one occasion he administered a severe rebuke to one of his followers because he stared and his eyes were lofty. The disciple, much affected by this reproof, changed his manner entirely and became so humble that, whereas when he first came to the house the master and mistress had hurried to wait upon him, now the other guests did not hesitate to wrangle with him for a place to put their mats.

Beside being a teacher, Lao-tze held office under the Chow government. A stone tablet in his temple says that he was Curator of the Royal Library and later Recorder under the

Pillar. He also held other offices, but his experience as a public official was not a happy one. While the historical circumstances under which he lived are hardly referred to in his book, the little that he says shows clearly his dissatisfaction with social and political conditions. A saying attributed to him by one of his followers probably expresses accurately his opinion of the political conditions of his day: the rulers, he says, unlike those of olden times, exploit the people and require of them more than can be performed; as a result, "Insufficiency of strength produces hypocrisy; insufficiency of knowledge produces deception; insufficiency of means produces robbery." The responsibility for these crimes he lays upon the rulers. We know from other sources that the time was one of disorder and oppression, when thoughtful men felt little inclination to engage in political activity. The great dynasty of Chow was in a state of decadence, which so distressed the philosopher that he finally resigned his office and "lived in his own house."

Lao-tze has been severely criticized for thus withdrawing "into convenient irresponsibility" instead of endeavoring to reform the government, but to have done this would have been to violate his own convictions. He may have been mistaken, but we have no right to require that he should act according to ideals which he did not accept. While he was living in retirement, it is said, he was visited by Confucius. The young reformer wished to deposit some books in the royal library with which Lao-tze had been connected, and he was told that Lao-tze might help him, but for some unknown reason Lao-tze refused to do so. The efforts of Confucius to persuade him led to a discussion between the two sages, in the course of which Lao-tze rebuked the younger sage for "introducing disorder into the nature of man" by his efforts to reform society. The story illustrates Lao-tze's ideal, though it must be taken with several grains of salt, because the followers of Lao-tze were all too fond of telling tales in which the Master of the Confucianists appeared at a disadvantage in discussion with their own teacher. Some of these stories we shall have occasion to repeat in connection with Lao-tze's teaching.

For a while after he retired from office Lao-tze continued to reside at the capital of Chow, but at length he decided to withdraw from the kingdom altogether. Travelling, as was his wont, "in carriage by black oxen drawn," he approached the gate leading out of the kingdom to the Northwest. Here the keeper of the gate, recognizing him as "the True Man," stopped him and besought him before departing to leave a record of his teaching. It is said that he also set before the sage a dish of tea, and that this was the origin of tea-drinking between host and guest! In response to the man's request Lao-tze wrote his book, the Tao-Teh-King, then left for parts unknown. No man knows where he died. Sometimes it is said that he went to India and was there reborn as the Buddha.

In another story, quite inconsistent with all this, we find a crowd of mourners wailing about the corpse of Lao-tze. A wise man who has come to pay his respect to the memory of the departed sage, observing the extreme grief of the bereaved disciples, concludes that Lao-tze must have been only an ordinary man after all; otherwise he would not have so attached his followers to himself that his death would call forth such unphilosophical mourning.

Whatever may have been the actual manner of his death,

we have the book which he is said to have written for the gatekeeper, and it undoubtedly presents his teachings faithfully. It is a little book, even shorter than our Gospel of Mark, and the style is very condensed. A gift for epigrammatic expression is evident in sayings like this: "If you keep feeling a point that has been sharpened, the point cannot long preserve its sharpness." Brief as it is, the Tao-Teh-King has had much influence. It has been greatly admired in the West as well as in the East. A Roman Catholic missionary in the eighteenth century translated it into Latin, believing that it evinced an acquaintance with the Christian doctrines of the Trinity and the Incarnation. A French translator early in the nineteenth century thought he had found the name "Jehovah" in it and regarded its teaching as anticipating Pythagoras and Plato. Tolstoi is said to have been much influenced by it and to have contemplated a Russian translation.

The name Tao-Teh-King means "The Book of the Way and of Virtue." The conception of the "Way" (Tao) is the centre of all Lao-tze's teaching, and for this reason his religion is know as Taoism. Most of the personally founded religions are named after their founders, but this one gets its name from its leading idea. Perhaps Lao-tze was not in the strictest sense the founder of Taoism. The principles he taught may have been known before his day. But, as we have already remarked, no religion or philosophy is created out of nothing. The most original genius has a social heritage and owes much to his predecessors.

Christian missionaries have seen in the Tao a close resemblance to the conception of the Word in the Gospel of John, and so have translated, "In the beginning was the

Tao, and the Tao was with God, and the Tao was God." But, though we may say that in the thinking of Lao-tze the Tao takes the place of God, it is not God, nor would Lao-tze say that in the beginning it was with God—not, at least, if we mean by God the Heavenly Emperor, the Supreme Being of the old Chinese religion. Lao-tze mentions the Heavenly Emperor but once in the Tao-Teh-King, and then only to say that before even He existed, there was the Tao. Yet if we mean by the word God, not a personal Being, but the supreme power and governing principle of the universe, then we may rightly say that the Tao is God.

Literally the word means simply "a road" or "a way"; it is also used of a method, course, or manner of action, just as the Bible speaks of "the way of an eagle in the air, the way of a serpent upon a rock, the way of a ship in the midst of the sea, and the way of a man with a maid." We speak of the way a man lives, or the way a machine works. So Lao-tze, giving the term a cosmic application, thinks of the Tao as the way the universe works, both the law by which it runs and the power which operates through that law. Some scholars translate it as Reason, using that word in the sense in which the Stoic philosophers of Greece and Rome thought of the universe as governed by Reason. The Tao is the reality behind all appearances, the ultimate ground of being. We say the universe is governed by natural law. Some would say that this law is the way God works; others would say it is merely the working of blind Force. "Some call it Evolution, and others call it God." Lao-tze calls it the Tao. Perhaps, as many writers have suggested, the conception which in our thinking comes nearest to Lao-tze's idea of the Tao is the conception of nature, not in the narrower sense in which we speak of nature-study, but in the inclusive sense implied by such expressions as "the laws of nature." Wordsworth's adoration of nature is in some respects not unlike Lao-tze's adoration of the Tao, except that the element of esthetic enjoyment is not much in evidence in Lao-tze.

And as the Stoics said that man should live "according to nature," *i.e.,* according to the laws of the immanent, divine Reason, so Lao-tze held that man should live according to the Tao. Judaism and Christianity teach that human conduct should imitate the perfect righteousness of God. "Ye shall be holy, for I am holy," says the Old Testament. "Love your enemies," says Jesus, "bless them that curse you, do good to them that hate you, and pray for them which despitefully use you, and persecute you; that ye may be the children of your father which is in heaven: for he maketh his sun to rise on the evil and on the good, and sendeth rain on the just and on the unjust,"—in other words, the impartial bounty of nature is a model for human goodness. Lao-tze does not interpret the operations of heaven and earth as manifesting the goodness of a Heavenly Father, but he does see in them a pattern for human conduct. The way of the universe is also the true way of human life.

What this way is we shall consider under the head of Lao-tze's ethical ideals, but first we must ask how one is to discover it. Is it to be formulated scientifically through systematic observation, as the laws of physics and chemistry are formulated? Not at all. It can be known only by the inner experience of mystic vision. You do not have to leave home, Lao-tze says, nor even to look out of the window to see the Tao: "The farther that one goes out (from himself), the less he knows." And again, "The sages got their knowledge without travelling." This is in striking contrast to the saying of the later Hebrew sage, Ben Sira, that the wise man "will travel through the land of strange nations" in his search for knowledge; yet a Hebrew writer of about the time of Lao-tze attributed words much like his to Moses: "For this commandment which I command thee this day, it is not hidden from thee, Neither is it far off. It is not in heaven, that thou shouldest say, Who shall go up for us to heaven, and bring it unto us, that we may hear it and do it? Neither is it beyond the sea, that thou shouldest say, Who shall go over the sea for us, and bring it unto us, that we may hear it and do it? But the word is very nigh unto thee, in thy mouth, and in thy heart, that thou mayest do it." We are also reminded of what a Hebrew poet wrote about wisdom in the twenty-eighth chapter of Job, and of what the apostle Paul said concerning spiritual as against worldly wisdom in the opening chapters of the First Epistle to the Corinthians.

A few quotations from the Tao-Teh-King may help to clarify the meaning of the Tao. "There was something undefined and complete, coming into existence before Heaven and Earth. How still it was and formless, standing alone, and undergoing no change, reaching everywhere and in no danger (of being exhausted)! It may be regarded as the Mother of all things. I do not know its name, and I give it the designation of the Tao. Making an effort (further) to give it a name I call it The Great."

"The Tao, considered as unchanging, has no name."

"As soon as it proceeds to action, it has a name."

The conception of a twofold existence, the original unchanging and unnamed state and the derived existence which is changeable and has a name, recalls not only certain Hindu ideas but also the teaching of the Hellenistic Jewish philosopher Philo, a contemporary of Jesus, who wrote in similar terms of the Logos, the eternal Word of God.

The passages which have been quoted show plainly that Lao-tze was a mystic as well as a philosopher. The contrast between him and Confucius in this respect appears in many of the stories to which reference has already been made. We are told, for example, that one day when Lao-tze had just washed his hair and was drying it in the sun, Confucius came to see him and found him standing in a mystic trance, "motionless, and as if there were not another man in the world." Confucius waited until the elder sage returned to normal consciousness, then expressed his amazement at what he had seen. "Just now," he said, "your body, Sir, was like the stump of a rotten tree. You looked as if you had no thought of anything, as if you had left the society of man, and were standing in the solitude."

"I was enjoying myself," Lao-tze replied, "in thinking about the commencement of things."

At Confucius' request Lao-tze then told him about the origin of the world. Confucius asked him about his enjoyment in these thoughts, and Lao-tze described it as the greatest of all enjoyments, the suitable occupation of the perfect man. Then, in answer to an inquiry about the method of attaining this great joy, Lao-tze discoursed in terms that elicited the most superlative praise from Confucius but convey no particular meaning to the Occidental reader, except that life and death are matters of indifference to him who has the secret of the Tao.

In his mysticism we have the most striking feature of Lao-tze's personality. That he should be so unlike Confucius in this particular, is all the more remarkable because the traits in which Confucius differs from Lao-tze are characteristic of the Chinese people as a whole. The Chinese in general are orderly, systematic, and practical—not at all concerned with metaphysical problems or communion with the Unseen. Many writers have compared them with the Romans in this regard. So striking is the difference between this typical Chinese temperament and the unworldly mind of Lao-tze that some scholars have even doubted whether he was a native of China. Probably the truth is rather that the Chinese, like other peoples, are not all alike. The success of Buddhism in China is enough to show that many of them are capable of other interests than those which are apparent in Confucianism.

Several passages in the Tao-Teh-King show that Lao-tze regarded himself as different from his fellows. "The multitude of men look satisfied and pleased; as if enjoying a full banquet, as if mounted on a tower in spring. I alone seem listless and still, my desires having as yet given no indication of their presence. I am like an infant which has not yet smiled. I look dejected and forlorn, as if I had no home to go to. The multitude of men all have enough and to spare. I alone seem to have lost everything. My mind is that of a stupid man; I am in a state of chaos." . . . "Ordinary men look bright and intelligent, while I alone seem to be benighted. They look full of discrimination while I am dull and confused." . . . "All men have their spheres of action, while I alone am dull and incapable." . . . "I alone am different from other men." All this sounds like either biliousness or acute adolescence, but even if we suspect no gentle irony in it, the true mystic is likely to feel that he is different from other people, and that they do not understand him. And he is likely to be right.

The most famous of the stories of conversations between Lao-tze and Confucius—the only one of them, indeed, which is generally accepted as having an historical basis—is to the effect that in 517 B.C., when Confucius was in his thirty-fifth year and Lao-tze in his eighty-eighth, Confucius went to see Lao-tze in order to question him about ceremonies (a subject in which Confucius was more interested than Lao-tze seems to have been). Lao-tze told him that a superior man does not appear outwardly to be superior and urged him to put away his "proud air and many desires." After the interview Confucius remarked to his disciples that he could understand the ways of birds, fishes, and animals, but the dragon was incomprehensible—and he had just seen the dragon.

In a different account of what may have been the same interview Lao-tze, reproving Confucius for his "painful iteration of benevolence and righteousness" and his fruitless expenditure of energy, like going about with a drum to find a lost boy, continues in words that recall what Jesus said about the lilies of the field and the birds of the heaven: "The snow-goose does not bathe every day to make itself white, nor the crow blacken itself every day to make itself black. The natural simplicity of their black and white does not afford any ground for controversy; and the fame and praise which men like to contemplate do not make them greater than they naturally are."

After this interview Confucius is asked by his disciples how he has admonished and corrected the Old Philosopher. Comparing Lao-tze to the dragon as in the other story, Confucius says, "I kept my mouth open, and was unable to shut it;—how could I admonish and correct Lao-Tan?"

On another occasion, so the story goes, Confucius, "being at leisure," asked Lao-tze about the Tao. Lao-tze said to him, "You must, as by fasting and vigil, clear and purge your mind, wash your spirit white as snow, and sternly repress your knowledge." He added that the subject was deep and difficult but kindly condescended to offer "an outline of its simplest attributes."

After reading these stories it is reassuring to know that eventually Confucius succeeded in securing the approval of "the dragon." Once, we are told, Confucius complained that, after studying the six writings and discoursing with seventy-two rulers about the good examples given by the great emperors of antiquity, he had not found one who would adopt his teachings and put them into practice. Lao-tze replied that the books gave only footprints and not the shoes that produced them. "The nature cannot be altered," he said; "the conferred constitution cannot be changed; the march of the seasons cannot be arrested; the Tao cannot be stopped. If you get the Tao, there is no effect that cannot be produced; if you miss it, there is no effect that can." After this interview Confucius did not go out for three months; then he came back to Lao-tze and confessed that he had not been able to transform men because he had not been playing his part in harmony with the processes of nature. Thereupon Lao-tze said to him, "You will do. Khiu, you have found the Tao."

While Lao-tze differed in many respects, and very radically, from Confucius, the two were alike in looking backward to a Golden Age in the remote past. The society of his own day seemed to Lao-tze to be the result of a long process of decline and decay. In the earliest times men had the Tao, and then there was no need of government or even of virtue, for virtue is the opposite of vice and presupposes it. "When the Tao was lost, its attributes appeared; when its attributes were lost, benevolence appeared; when benevolence was lost, righteousness appeared; and when righteousness was lost, the proprieties appeared."

And Lao-tze had an explanation for the degeneration of mankind. All the evils of society he traced to the pursuit of knowledge. In the Golden Age men were virtuous without knowing it. We are reminded of a familiar story from another Oriental people which attributes the entrance of sin into the world to man's eating the fruit of the tree of the knowledge of good and evil. "If we could renounce our sageness and discard our wisdom," says the Tao-Teh-King, "it would be better for the people a hundredfold. If we could renounce our benevolence and discard righteousness, the people would again become filial and kindly. If we could renounce our artful contrivances and discard our (scheming for) gain, there would be no thieves nor robbers." To some extent one can sympathize with this point of view. Simple innocence and lack of self-seeking are beautiful, and the search for truth has not always been for the good of mankind. It was Jesus who said, "I thank thee, Father, Lord of heaven and earth, that thou didst hide these things from the wise and understanding, and didst reveal them unto babes." And the apostle Paul wrote to the Corinthians, "God chose the foolish things of the world, that he might put to shame them that are wise." Lao-tze may have exaggerated when he wrote, "When we renounce learning we have no troubles," but there was a Hebrew sage also who said, "He that increaseth knowledge increaseth sorrow."

Lao-tze did not hesitate to draw the practical conclusion from this that a wise government would keep its people ignorant. He was asked, "If you do not govern the world, how can you make men's minds good?"

"Take care how you meddle with and disturb men's minds," he replied. "The mind, if pushed about, gets depressed; if helped forward, it gets exalted."

Government and education are not the only activities discouraged by Lao-tze. Any form of self-seeking is condemned. "There is no guilt greater than to sanction ambition; no calamity greater than to be discontented with one's lot." Here again, if we think Lao-tze exaggerates, we may be reminded of Paul's statement, "I have learned in whatsoever state I am, therewith to be content." But Paul was a man of action, and Lao-tze would have rebuked him as he rebuked Confucius. He who is devoted to the Tao, he says, instead of seeking to increase his knowledge, seeks to diminish his doings, until he reaches the point of complete non-action. When he arrives at this point, "there is nothing which he does not do." So far as practical life is concerned, that is the fundamental principle of Taoism—non-action. "The violent wind does not last for a whole morning; a sudden rain does not last for a whole day. . . . If Heaven and Earth cannot make such (spasmodic) actings last long, how much less can man!" "The violent and strong do not die their natural death. I will make this the basis of my teaching." Again we are reminded of Ecclesiastes: "The race is not to the swift nor the battle to the strong." But Ecclesiastes does not draw the inference that all is done by doing nothing; his conclusion is that "time and chance happeneth to them all."

Among the stories of conversations between Lao-tze and Confucius is one which, like most of them, is probably unhistorical and yet seems to reflect the true spirit of Lao-tze. It pictures Confucius in his fifty-first year (when Lao-tze would be over a hundred years old) as coming to see Lao-tze, who greets him with the words, "You have come, Sir, have you? I have heard that you are the wisest man of the North; have you also got the Tao?" Confucius admits that he has sought it in various ways but has not found it. Lao-tze tells him that it can be given only when the mind has the inner power to receive it. Fame and wealth are not worth seeking. Even benevolence and righteousness should be, as they were for the kings of old, only lodging-houses for a night. "The perfect men of old trod the path of benevolence as a path which they borrowed for the occasion, and dwelt in righteousness as in a lodging which they used for a night. Thus they rambled in the vacancy of Untroubled Ease, found their food in the fields of Indifference, and stood in the gardens which they had not borrowed. Untroubled Ease requires the doing of nothing; Indifference is easily supplied with nourishment; not borrowing needs no outlay. The ancients called this the Enjoyment that Collects the True."

This ideal for human life, as we have seen, is drawn from the contemplation of nature. The Way of the universe is the right Way for man. Water is strong by being weak; the soft overcomes the hard and the weak the strong. To a man who asks how to regulate his life Lao-tze says, "Can you hold the One Thing fast in your embrace?" This brings to mind the saying, "But one thing is needful." And there is a still more striking reminder of Jesus' words in the question with which Lao-tze continues: "Can you become a little child?" He goes on to explain that a child's constitution is in perfect harmony: it can cry all day without getting hoarse. "The little child moves unconscious of what it is doing, and walks unconscious of whither it is going." So the perfect man is not troubled by considerations of advantage and disadvantage, makes no plans, and lives in utter simplicity. The idea of becoming like little children appears in the Tao-Teh-King as well as in this later anecdote.

Naturally humility is a virtue much emphasized by Laotze. Just as the Tao pervades all things, and all are dependent upon it, yet it claims no credit and exerts no authority, so the sage is able to accomplish great things by not making himself great. Heaven and earth endure because they do not live of or for themselves; so the sage puts himself last. Rivers and streams receive tribute from the valley streams by being lower than they are; so the sage is above others because he puts himself below them. One must overcome himself: "He who overcomes others is strong; he who overcomes himself is mighty." One must empty himself: the use of a wheel depends on the hole for the axle; the use of vessels of clay depends upon the hollow space inside them; so is it also with doors and windows and the space inside a room. "The man who has forgotten himself is he of whom it is said that he has become identified with Heaven."

With humility goes gentleness, unfailing kindness. Here Lao-tze rises to a higher moral level than any other teacher outside of Christianity. "Recompense injury with kindness," he says in no uncertain terms. "To those who are good to me, I am good; to those who are not good to me, I am also good. And thus all get to be good." We have already noted that Jesus too based his exhortation to love our enemies on the undiscriminating bounty of nature.

Lao-tze's ideal is inconsistent with such an institution as war, and it is striking to find a teacher at such an early date putting himself on record as definitely as Lao-tze does in this regard. "There is no calamity greater," he says, "than lightly engaging in war." . . . "When the Tao prevails in the world, they send back their swift horses to (draw) the dung-carts. When the Tao is disregarded in the world, the war-horses breed in the border lands." . . . "He who will assist a lord of men in harmony with the Tao will not assert his mastery in the kingdom by force of arms. Such a course is sure to meet with its proper return." . . . "In the sequence of great armies there are sure to be bad years."

A striking comparison is drawn in one passage of the Tao-Teh-King. On festive occasions, says Lao-tze, the place of honor is on the left hand, while in the rites of mourning it is on the right; therefore it is fitting that the general's place in the army is on the right side, for mourning becomes him rather than rejoicing. Legge compares with this the remark of the Duke of Wellington "that to gain a battle was the saddest thing next to losing it." We may also recall the saying of Jesus, "For all they that take the sword shall perish by the sword."

The Tao is not only a way to follow; it is also a possession to covet and to cherish. Some of Lao-tze's sayings are
not unlike what Jesus said about the Kingdom of Heaven
as the pearl of great price and the treasure for which a man
will sell all that he has, also his words about laying up
treasure in heaven and about the futility of gaining the
whole world if one loses his own soul. A poetical passage
in the Tao-Teh-King is rendered in English verse as follows:

> "Or fame or life,
>   Which do you hold more dear?
> Or life or wealth,
>   To which would you adhere?
> Keep life and lose these other things;
> Keep them and lose your life:—which brings
>   Sorrow and pain more near?"

The possession of the Tao is so great a boon that Lao-tze
makes extravagant statements about the powers it confers
upon him who has it. He who has the Tao, he says, need
not fear wild beasts, birds of prey, or poisonous insects.
This statement has been criticized as contrary to all experience, yet we read in the Old Testament, "Thou shalt not
be afraid for the terror by night, nor for the arrow that
flieth by day; for the pestilence that walketh in darkness,
nor for the destruction that wasteth at noonday." And the
New Testament promises to "them that believe" that "they
shall take up serpents, and if they drink any deadly thing,
it shall in no wise hurt them."

It may be, however, that such promises gave some excuse
for the sad spiritual degeneration which took place among
the later Taoists. Some of Lao-tze's followers were, like

himself, sages and philosophers, but the mass of them became interested chiefly in seeking the elixir of life and the
so-called philosopher's stone. They cared more for avoiding death and for changing lead into gold than they did for
finding the great secret of life, the eternal Way of the universe, and patterning their conduct after it. It is even said
that one of the later emperors of China was so eager for the
elixir of life that he took an overdose and died of it! Legge
suggests that before Lao-tze there may have been Taoists
who, like those of later centuries, were concerned primarily
with the prolongation of life, and that Lao-tze may have
tried to raise them to the higher spiritual level of his own
teaching.

However this may have been, it is clear that Lao-tze did
not found a religion in the sense that Mohammed or Zoroaster did. He did not establish an organization to spread his
teaching. The Chinese historian to whom we owe the story
of the composition of the Tao-Teh-King says that Lao-tze's
great desire was "to keep himself concealed and remain unknown." He had nothing to say of worship, temples, ritu-
als, and priests; he was even agnostic as regards God. The
Chinese term which is commonly translated as God occurs
only once in the Tao-Teh-King. Speaking of the Tao, Lao-
tze says, "I do not know whose Son it is; it might seem to
be before God." Another term, meaning Heaven, is used
often, but in a sense which makes it little more than an ad-
jective: "the Tao of Heaven" is spoken of in contrast with
"the Tao of man." A remark attributed to Lao-tze is notable in this connection, though its genuineness is decidedly
doubtful. Discoursing with Confucius about the beginnings
of things on one of the occasions of which we have already

spoken, Lao-tze refers to the Chinese conception of the primeval states of the universe, Yin and Yang, and says, "The two states communicating together, a harmony ensued and things were produced. Some one regulated and controlled all this, but no one has seen his form." Strictly speaking, Lao-tze was a philosopher rather than a religious leader, a sage rather than a prophet, yet his teaching has much in common with some of the most profound ideas and most lofty ideals of the greatest religions. Furthermore, as has been abundantly evident, he was not only a thinker; he was a mystic, finding in union with the Tao the way to abiding peace and joy. In this sense the Taoism of Lao-tze was a religion and a much nobler religion than the organized Taoism of later times.

Chapter Three

CONFUCIUS

REFORMER AND TEACHER

Lao-tze's younger contemporary, Confucius, whom we have already met while making the acquaintance of the Taoist sage, was born in the state of Lu, in what is now the province of Shantung, in the year 551 b.c. His family was of noble extraction; indeed some writers trace his ancestry to the mythical emperor Huang Ti, who is supposed to have been one of the founders of the empire. In former days his ancestors had enjoyed high rank in a neighboring state, but a reversal of fortune had compelled them to take refuge in Lu, where now for several generations they had held positions with the government.

In spite of his high origin, Confucius' early life was not an easy one. The youngest of eleven children, he was only three years old when his father died, and he had to help support them all by hard manual labor. In later years he said that this early necessity had given him a mastery of many accomplishments which were of no use to a "superior man." At the age of nineteen he married. A son was born to him, and also, it seems, a daughter, for we read of his giving her in marriage to a man of whom he said that "though imprisoned, he had committed no crime."

It is often alleged that Confucius' married life was unhappy, and even that it ended in a divorce, but the statement is based on mere inference from passages which do not definitely imply it, and on the interpretation of which even native commentators are not agreed. To be sure, when Confucius' wife died, and his son continued to mourn her death for more than a year (the recognized time of mourning for parents), the sage rebuked him. But that does not necessarily indicate any lack of esteem for the departed wife. Confucius was punctilious about mourning customs, as he was about all customs. Other instances are on record of his rebuking those who mourned beyond the set time. On the other hand he once commended a man whose grief was so great that he did not resume his former pleasures even when the period of mourning was ended; indeed we are told that Confucius himself felt such lasting grief, presumably for the loss of his own mother, that when the year of mourning was over he still did not handle his lute for five days, and then could not bring perfect tones from it. Only after ten days did he play on the organ and sing.

Whatever may have been his relations with his wife, he was a stern father to his son. The latter was once asked what he had learned from his father. He replied, "He was standing alone once . . . and said to me, 'Have you learned the Odes?' On my replying 'Not yet,' he added, 'If you do not learn the Odes, you will not be fit to converse with.' I retired and studied the Odes. Another day he . . . said to me, 'Have you learned the rules of Propriety?' On my replying 'Not yet,' he added, 'If you do not learn the rules of Propriety, your character cannot be established.' I then retired, and studied the rules of Propriety." On hearing this the man who had inquired about the young man's training expressed great satisfaction: it showed, he declared, that "the superior man maintains a distant reserve towards his son."

In order to support his family Confucius accepted a government position as keeper of the stores of grain, but at the age of twenty-two he was released from this office in order to take up the work of a teacher. He established a private school and became so well known that students came to him in large numbers, including some of the nobility. In his thirty-fifth year he made a visit to the capital of the empire, investigated the history of the ruling dynasty, and looked at the famous altars to heaven and earth.

It was at this time that he is supposed to have had the famous conversation with Lao-tze which led him to compare the older sage to a dragon. In the previous chapter we found that the Taoist scriptures contain many stories of interviews between Lao-tze and Confucius. In one of the Confucian books there is a story to the effect that the two sages once assisted together at a funeral. During the ceremony an eclipse of the sun occurred, and their opinions differed on the question of stopping the rites while it lasted. Confucius did as Lao-tze directed but afterward respectfully questioned him about the reasons for his action.

The number of Confucius' pupils, it is said, increased after his visit to the capital, but a year or two later the political affairs of the state of Lu were so disturbed that the ruler under whom Confucius had served was driven into exile and Confucius followed him. In another province Confucius found employment as the steward of a mandarin. He was introduced to the prince, who after conversing with him about the relations of ruler and minister, and of father and son, was minded to give him a position in the government, but was dissuaded by his counsellors, who said that Confucius belonged to the sect of the Learned, "a conceited, unmanageable group."

The following year Confucius went back to Lu but did not accept office, holding that the men in power had unlawfully seized the reins of government. Instead of public service he turned to literary work, undertaking to revise the ancient classics and also the art of music. This work did not occupy him entirely, however, for students came to him again in large numbers and from all directions. About fifteen years were spent thus in teaching and scholarly research. When he was fifty-one years old he again entered public life as chief magistrate of a town.

As we observed in studying the life of Lao-tze, there was much political and social disorder in China at this time. According to Mencius, one of the greatest Confucian writers, "There were ministers who murdered their rulers and sons who murdered their fathers." No strong central government existed to keep order between the nobles, who in true feudal fashion warred among themselves. Confucius bewailed the lack of law and order: "The Western and Northern barbarians have rulers," he said, "and are not like us, the multitudes of China, who have lost them." . . . "I have seen the day when the imperial historian would leave a blank in the record when he was not sure of the date; and when he who had a horse would lend it to another. Such days are gone."

Naturally the people suffered most from the prevailing anarchy and violence. They had no interest in the wars of rival barons, but they were forced nevertheless to fight for one or the other, and neither their lives nor their property were safe. Once, it is said, Confucius found a woman sitting in a lonely spot and wailing. He asked what it was that troubled her, and she explained that both her husband and her son had been killed there by tigers. When asked why she continued to live in such a place, she replied, "Here there is no oppressive ruler." The sage turned to his followers and said: "Remember this: oppressive rule is more cruel than a tiger."

In view of such conditions it is not surprising that Confucius re-entered the political arena with considerable hesitation. He seems to have had the feeling, which keeps many good men out of politics nowadays, that he who handles pitch will be defiled. Either at this time or at some other period, when his services were sought by a government of which he did not approve, he avoided the official who came to speak to him on the subject. The latter thereupon sent him a pig as a present. Courtesy required that Confucius should call upon the giver to thank him for his gift; he chose a day when the official was away from home, but as luck would have it, the two met on the street. The official said to him, "Is it right for a man to leave his jewel in his bosom and leave his country in confusion?"

"No," said Confucius.

"Can he be called wise," continued the official, "who is anxious to be engaged in public employment, and yet is constantly losing the opportunity to do so?"

"No," said Confucius.

"The days and months are passing," said the official; "the years do not wait for us."

"Right," said Confucius; "I will go into office."

There were others also who felt that a good man could

not serve such a government. Several stories are told of men who by word or deed made plain their disapproval of the sage's conduct, but he said, "I cannot associate with birds and beasts. If I follow not men, whom shall I follow?" One of his followers defended him by saying, "Personal purity must be sacrificed to duty."

The results he achieved would seem to justify his confidence that he could improve matters by taking an active part in the government. From the office of chief magistrate in a town he rose to the position of superintendent of public works for the state. In this capacity he introduced important improvements in agriculture. Later he became minister of justice, and as such is said to have abolished crime in the state. So great was the progress effected by him in the government of Lu that a neighboring state became alarmed and adopted a mean expedient to force Confucius out of office. A troupe of chorus girls was sent as a present to the prince of Lu; as the givers hoped, he was so entranced by them that for three days he neglected the affairs of the state entirely. The disgusted Confucius, as Professor G. F. Moore puts it, "sadly—and slowly, hoping that the duke might at last repent—shook the dust of the ungrateful state from his feet."

After his resignation Confucius visited some of the neighboring states. In one place, mistaken by the people for a tyrant against whom they were enraged, he was in grave danger, but he calmly asserted that Heaven had entrusted to him the cause of truth, and the people could not hurt him. For thirteen years he wandered about with a band of disciples, unable to find a ruler who would employ him. Finally, at the age of sixty-eight, he again returned to Lu.

He did not, however, enter public life again. The closing years of his life were devoted to literary labors, compiling the Classics and composing his only original production, *Spring and Autumn,* a history of the state of Lu.

Disappointment clouded these last years. None of the rulers of his day would accept him as counsellor and put his teachings into effect in the administration of government. One day, when he was seventy-two years old, he rose early and walked slowly about before his door, singing,

> "The great mountain must crumble;
> "The strong beam must break;
> "The wise man must wither away like a plant."

When he re-entered his room and sat down, his servant, who had heard his sad singing, expressed a fear that his master was going to be ill. Confucius spoke to him of the ways in which the people of different places buried their dead, and added, "I am a descendant of Yin and last night I dreamed that I was sitting with the offerings to the dead by my side between the two pillars. Intelligent kings do not arise; and what one under heaven is going to take me as his Master? I apprehend I am about to die." What the servant had feared came to pass, and after a week's illness the venerable sage breathed his last. For three years his disciples mourned him; one indeed remained six years at the grave.

In sharp contrast to Lao-tze's policy of withdrawal and inaction Confucius strove by actual administration, by counselling rulers, by writing, and by teaching to bring about the reformation he desired to see. As an administrator he was remarkably successful: all too successful, as we have seen, for his phenomenal achievements brought about his downfall as a public official. As an adviser of rulers he accomplished little, because the rulers would not follow his advice. He was not the last professor of political science to have difficulty in getting his theories adopted by hard-headed administrators. It is as a writer that he has exerted the greatest influence on posterity, yet he cannot be classed as a great author. Most of his literary work was done in the capacity of an editor, and the little that we have from his own pen shows no particular literary gift—least of all originality, the last thing he would have wanted it to show. "I compile and transmit to posterity," he said, "but write not any new thing. I believe and love the ancients."

As far as special gifts are concerned, Confucius was above all else a great teacher. He attracted students from far and near and bound them to himself with the bonds of loyalty and devotion. All he required of those who would study under him was an earnest purpose. "From the man bringing his bundle of dried flesh for my teaching upwards, I have never refused instruction to any one," he said. He expected his pupils to do their part, however. "He who does not exert his mind," he said, "I do not explain matters to him; he who does not exert his mouth, I do not assist him to express himself. When I help a man around one corner, if he does not get around the other three, I do not again assist him."

Evidently he wished his students to reflect upon his teaching. "Learning without thought," he said, "is labor lost; thought without learning is perilous." Not only reflection but also practical application was expected. "Although a man may be able to recite the three hundred odes, if, when he receives an appointment, he knows not how to act, or when sent abroad as an ambassador, he is unable to answer the questions put to him, of what use is his learning?" Of one of his favorite disciples he said, "I have talked with Hwuy for a whole day, and he has not made any objection to anything I said;—as if he were stupid. He has retired, and I have examined his conduct when away from me, and found him able to illustrate my teachings. Hwuy!—He is not stupid." Again, "Straightforward language (or reproof), will not men assent to it? But it is reformation which is valuable. Insinuating words, will not men be pleased with them? But to investigate the source of the evil is the grand point. What can I do with those who are pleased and do not probe the root of the evil—who assent and do not reform?" Confucius, it would seem, had the same difficulty that the prophet Ezekiel is said to have experienced in Babylon a few decades earlier: "And, lo, thou art unto them as a very lovely song of one that hath a pleasant voice, and can play well on an instrument; for they hear thy words, but they do them not." Half a millennium later another teacher said, "And why call ye me, Lord, Lord, and do not the things which I say?"

Confucius' teaching activity was not restricted to the classroom. Once, it is said, he was conducting an archery meeting and made use of the opportunity to teach the people. One of his students described Confucius' method of teaching as follows: "My master led me gradually on, expanded my mind by learning and bound me by the knowledge of propriety." Sometimes he answered questions in a rather cryptic fashion which provoked further questioning.

To a student who asked him about virtue he replied, "The man of perfect virtue is slow and cautious in his speech."

" 'Slow and cautious!' Is that what is meant by perfect virtue?"

"When a man feels the difficulty of doing," said Confucius, "can he be other than cautious and slow in speaking?"

Like all great teachers, Confucius respected his students. "A young student," he said, "may be worthy of veneration. Who knows but his knowledge may yet equal mine? But," he added, "if a man arrive at forty, or fifty, without having acquired knowledge, he can never be worthy of veneration." He also adapted his teaching to the needs and capacity of the individual. When two disciples asked whether they should immediately carry into practice what they heard, Confucius told one of them to ask first the advice of his father and brother; to the other he said, "Act immediately." Asked why he gave them such different answers, he said, "The first man has more than his own share of energy. Therefore I kept him back. The second is retiring and slow; therefore I urged him forward." Sometimes, however, he seems to have talked over his students' heads. One of his followers said, "The virtue and elegant manners of our master, we may attain knowledge of; but his lectures on the nature of man, and divine reason, we cannot comprehend."

Yet there was no arrogant pride of learning in Confucius. "I have no knowledge," he said, "but if an ignorant person make inquiries, although he appear perfectly empty, I show him all the bearings and fully explain the sense of his questions." The statement might have come from Socrates! In accordance with this modesty, Confucius had the rare gift of restraint. He did not expect to be heard for his much speaking. Once, for example, he said, "I feel not inclined to speak." One of his disciples remonstrated: "If our master speak not, what will his pupils have to transmit to posterity?" Confucius answered, "Does Heaven speak? The four seasons pursue their courses, and all things are continually being produced, but does Heaven say anything?"

Like every true scholar, Confucius combined with his consciousness of ignorance a passionate desire for knowledge. His delight in learning is expressed in the very first sentence of the *Analects,* a book of his sayings compiled by his disciples. Elsewhere he is quoted as saying, "In a village of ten houses, there may be those who equal Mow [a name he often used to designate himself] in fidelity and sincerity, but not in his love of learning." When one of his followers was asked about his master's conduct and declined to reply, Confucius said, "Why did you not say that he is a man who in his zeal to obtain knowledge forgets to eat, and in his joy on having obtained it forgets the anxiety it cost him, and that he is insensible to the approach of old age." He also said of himself, "I was not born with knowledge. I love the ancients and study them with diligence that I may obtain knowledge." His progress in learning he described as follows: "At fifteen I was bent on study; at thirty my mind was firmly established; at forty I had no doubts; at fifty I understood the ways of heaven, and at seventy the wishes of my heart passed not the proper limits." Another saying expresses eloquently his scholarly aspirations: "To meditate on what one has learned, to learn without satiety, and teach without being wearied,—how can I attain to these!" And as he expected his students to put his teachings into practice, so he endeavored to govern his own conduct according to rational principles. "To act without knowing on what principle I am acting," he said, "is what I never do. I hear much, select what is good, and practise it; see much and remember what is seen."

To music as well as scholarship Confucius was ardently devoted. When he heard the music of Shun, it is said, for three months he "knew not the taste of flesh." "I had no idea," he exclaimed, "that music, at its best, had arrived at this pitch." We are told that when he met any one who sang well, he had him repeat the piece he had sung and then joined him in singing it. We have already seen that he reformed the practice of music in Lu. He believed that music had an important effect upon character and conduct. In response to an inquiry regarding the right way to govern a province he said, "Follow the divisions of time made by the Hea dynasty, ride in the carriages of Yin, wear the diadem of Chow, use the music of Shun. But beware the music of Chin and put loquacious flatterers at a distance, for the music of Chin is licentious, and flatterers are dangerous." References to his own playing and singing and his remarks upon the performances of others abound in the accounts of his life. One example of his keenness as a music-critic may be cited. Hearing a certain instrumental and vocal performance, he smiled and made a remark which might well be applied to some of our modern occidental music, with its clumsy straining after effects: "When you kill a fowl, why use a knife employed to slay an ox?"

If Confucius was humble with regard to his scholarly attainments, he was still more so with regard to his character, as the following sayings make plain: "In learning I am equal to others, but I cannot by any means exhibit the man of superior virtue in my conduct." "There are three things in the practice of the superior man to which I cannot reach: virtuous, he is free from anxieties; wise, he is free from perplexities; bold, he is free from fear. . . . In the way of the superior man there are four things to which I have not yet attained. To serve my father as I would require my son to serve me, to serve my ruler as I would require my minister to serve me, to serve an elder brother as I would require a younger brother to serve me, to set an example in behaving to a friend as I would require him to behave to me I am not able." Similarly, after instructing his followers when they went out to serve the prince and his minister, when at home to serve their fathers and elder brothers, in funeral and sacrificial rites not to do their utmost, and in drinking not to indulge so far as to confuse their minds, he added, "How can I lay claim to such conduct?" To infer from the last part of this that he was actually intemperate is unwarranted. It is explicitly stated by one of his followers that while he used wine more freely than rice or meat, he never drank to the point of befuddling his wits. His humility and his common sense as well are further shown by the significant fact that he claimed no supernatural powers and refused to practise magic.

Many descriptions of the sage's personal traits and manners of life are given in the Confucian scriptures. He is said to have been "void of selfishness, prejudice, bigotry, and egotism." He was "mild, yet firm; majestic, but not harsh; grave, yet pleasant." When he was seated, "his manner was easy, thus, and his countenance benign, thus."

When he wished to obtain information, he did not seek it by direct inquiry:—"Our master is benign, upright, respectful, polite, and condescending: by these he obtains information. His mode of inquiring differs from that of other men."

With all his urbanity, he could on occasion express his opinions very frankly and directly. When a specious excuse was given for an action which he had condemned, he said dryly, "I hate loquacity." When one of his followers defended a shortcoming by saying that he delighted in his master's doctrine, but his strength was insufficient, Confucius replied, "Those whose strength is not sufficient go half way and then fail, but you are feigning." Of another disciple, who slept in the daytime, he said, "Rotten wood cannot be carved, a wall of dirty earth cannot be whitened."

His punctiliousness in all matters of custom is often represented as the dominant note in the personality of Confucius. Some writers find his character epitomized in the sentence, "If his mat were not straight he would not sit on it." It is true that when an objection was raised to the sacrificial slaughter of a lamb, he said, "I am concerned about the custom, not about the lamb." The circumstantial descriptions given of his clothing and diet show that either he or his followers attached considerable importance to these matters. His elaborate courtesy and meticulous conformity to the traditional rules for all occasions are evident at every turn. At the same time he also exhibited no little independence in the observance of the customs. Though strict etiquette prescribed a cap of fine linen, he accepted on the ground of economy the popular fashion of wearing a silk cap. On the other hand the prevailing practice of ascending the steps before bowing to the prince, instead of doing obeisance below stairs, as tradition required, was rejected by the sage because it seemed to him an expression of pride. "I will follow the custom of bowing below," he said, "although I should differ from all."

As a matter of fact, Confucius was not the kind of man to carry his punctiliousness to ridiculous extremes. He had too much sense of humor for that. A quiet, dry kind of humor it was, but its presence is unmistakable. To an over-conscientious follower who always considered a course of action three times before adopting it Confucius said, "Twice will do." Another remark will be appreciated by observers of our own times who have marked how much more easily fame is won by athletic prowess than by intellectual achievement. When someone complained that Confucius, with all his learning, had done nothing to make himself famous, he said, "What shall I bend my attention to? Shall I become a charioteer or an archer? I will become a charioteer!" The humorous aspect of another occasion may have been unintended, but more probably was not. When an undesired visitor came to his door, Confucius sent word that he was too ill to receive company, but even as the message was being delivered he played on his harp where the caller could plainly hear him. One would like to know whether the man was wise enough to take the hint.

Indications of normal human feelings and interests are not hard to find in the story of Confucius' life. He was fond of archery, hunting, and riding. And he was a true sportsman, for we read that he fished, but never used a net, and shot birds, but only on the wing. He could sympathize with the hilarious relaxation of unsophisticated folk on a festive occasion. Once a disciple scornfully said that the people at an annual agricultural sacrifice seemed to be mad, whereupon Confucius replied, "For their hundred days' labor in the fields, the men receive this one day's enjoyment from the state. Even Wan and Wu [famed emperors of the past] could not keep a bow in good condition if it were always drawn and never relaxed. To keep it strung and then unstrung was the way of Wan and Wu."

Like a later teacher in another land, Confucius was not afraid of being criticized for the company he kept. One of his followers once ventured to remonstrate with him for accepting an invitation from a man who was a rebel, but Confucius said, "If a thing be really hard, it may be ground without being made thin, and if it is white, it may be steeped in dark fluid without making it black. Am I a gourd? How can I be hung up out of the way of being eaten?" His reply to those who criticized him for accepting office under a corrupt government may be recalled in this connection.

Underlying all his interest in forms and institutions was a genuine concern for the welfare of the people. When one of his disciples expressed a desire for carriages, horses, and fine skin robes to share with his friends, and another said that what he most desired was the virtue of humility, Confucius said, "I wish to give ease to the old, to be faithful to friends, and to cherish the young." The depth of his fellow feeling for people in trouble is often manifest. In the company of one who had been bereaved he always ate sparingly, and he never sang on a day during which he had expressed sympathy for another's grief. Even the death of his dog is recorded as evoking a pathetic concern for a proper burial. Once, when an old friend had lost his mother, Confucius helped him make preparations for the funeral. In the midst of this solemn task the friend, perhaps crazed by his grief, stood upon the coffin and began to sing. Confucius paid no attention to the man, and when his disciples urged him to come away from such a scandalous situation he said to them, "I have heard that relations should not forget their relationship nor old acquaintances their friendship." Another demonstration of a courtesy far deeper than mere formality is to be seen in the case of a blind musician who joined a group in which Confucius was sitting. The sage arose and led the blind man to a seat, telling him, as they went, where the steps were and who was sitting here and there.

In religion, as in human relationships, Confucius was devoted to form and ceremony. Even as a child, it is said, he used to make imitations of the sacred vessels and play at carrying out the ceremonies. But here again he did not value form for its own sake. He regarded religious rites, like the conventional usages of polite social intercourse, as expressing an underlying spirit. Just how and why he emphasized the ceremonial side of religion we shall see in discussing his teaching. We shall also consider in that connection his religious beliefs, but we must note here, as a fundamental element in his character, his reverent attitude toward the unseen world. While, as we have already discovered, he was no mystic, we shall find that he was not without a real and profound religious faith.

Coming now to his teaching, we are prepared by what we know of his life and character to expect a type of thought very different from that of Lao-tze. Confucius was not a seeker after the hidden reality behind the world of appearances. To be sure, we have met with a reference to his obscure "lectures on the nature of man and divine reason," but whatever this means, his discourse was not at all like what we found in the Tao-Teh-King. Metaphysical and theological problems had no place in his teaching, either with beginners or with his most advanced students. "You suppose," he once said, "I have some mysterious doctrines, which I conceal from you. I have no secrets. Whatever I do, all is open to your view." When asked about the meaning of the great imperial sacrifices, he said, "I do not know. To him who knows this, everything under heaven is as plain as this:"—laying his finger in the palm of his hand. To an inquirer about serving the spirits of the departed he replied, "While you are not able to serve men, how can you serve their spirits?" The inquirer continued, "I venture to ask about death." "While you do not know life," said Confucius, "how can you know about death?"

Since he avoided such questions, it is impossible to know what he believed about them. In general we may say that he handed on the religion of the ancients, which was a combination of ancestor worship and nature worship. Heaven, the Supreme Emperor, and Earth were worshipped by the emperor as the Son of Heaven; below these were innumerable minor deities and spirits, including former rulers and other great men of the past. Heaven was thought of not only as the sky but as the moral order of the world, guiding human destiny, rewarding the good, and punishing the evil. Much of this Confucius simply took for granted; his teaching was primarily concerned with other matters.

It must not be supposed, however, that religious belief was wholly a matter of tradition and assumption with Confucius. We have said that he had a profound and genuine faith. Some of the old beliefs he may have doubted or rejected; others were very real to him. The conception of Heaven as the ground and guardian of the moral law not only underlay all his teaching; it was a source of personal comfort and assurance. He regarded his own mission as divinely ordained, and calmly faced danger in the assurance that Heaven would not allow him to perish until his work was done. Once, when he was very ill, one of his disciples urged him to pray. "Is it right that I should?" asked the sage. The disciple assured him that it was, quoting from one of the scriptures, to which Confucius replied, "Mow has prayed long." Whether this means that prayer was his usual practice, or, as some hold, that he regarded a righteous life as the truest prayer, cannot be determined. Less ambiguous is another saying which is frequently quoted. Feeling, as great souls so often feel, "despised and rejected of men" in spite of his great fame, Confucius said, "Alas, there is no one that knows me. I murmur not against heaven. I grumble not against men. My studies lie low, and my penetration rises high. But there is heaven; that knows me." In accordance with this faith Confucius is quoted as expressing wonder at the vast influence of the spirits, which fill everything, and this is his description of what constitutes true knowledge: "To perform fully the duties due to men, to reverence the gods, and keep at a due distance from them." Compare with this the Hebrew proverb, "The fear of the Lord is the beginning of wisdom," and the words of the prophet, "What doth the Lord require of thee, but to do justly, and to love mercy, and to walk humbly with thy God?" If Confucius was an agnostic, his agnosticism was not incompatible with reverence and a certain measure of assured religious faith.

In fact, on one point, which became a bone of contention between later Confucian philosophers and their opponents, Confucius had faith amounting almost to credulity. Heaven, he taught, not only governed human life in accordance with the moral law but gave mankind a disposition naturally inclined toward the right. Human nature was essentially good, and there was no Original Sin or hereditary depravity to prevent righteous living. The importance of this belief can hardly be exaggerated: it throws the responsibility for vice and crime upon environment and education, and conversely gives assurance that good education and example will surely succeed. Here is faith indeed.

With regard to ritual and ceremony Confucius was religious to a fault. Whereas Lao-tze, absorbed in metaphysical and mystical contemplation, despised all ritual, Confucius was as devoted to the ancient ceremonies as he was unconcerned about theology. His agnosticism as regards the objects of worship did not interfere with his insistence that the rites should be faithfully and properly performed. In this he only exhibited the characteristic disposition of the Chinese people as a whole, as we remarked in contrasting him with Lao-tze in the last chapter. We have also observed, however, that what he desired was not form for form's sake. If there was to be any excess, he taught, it should be in the spirit rather than in the form of the rite, and if there was to be any deficiency, it should be in the ritual rather than in the reverence with which it was performed. Economy in the conduct of all ceremonies was preferable to extravagance. Offerings to ancestors or to the gods should be made as though they were present: "I do not worship as if I were not worshipping." The great value of the ceremonies in Confucius' eyes, however, was not their efficacy in obtaining blessings from gods or ancestors but their effect upon the worshippers themselves. In the art of government as practised by the ancients he believed that the ruling principle was love of men, that the ceremonial rules provided the means of regulating this love of men, and that reverence was the essential element in the ceremonies. Thus religion was to Confucius an integral part of the established social system and valuable as such regardless of its philosophical implications.

The nature and scope of Confucius' interests may be seen in the list of the subjects which he taught: "history, poetry, literature, proprieties, government, natural science, music"; or, as they are elsewhere given, "literature, virtuous practices, faithfulness, and sincerity." He avoided "prodigies, feats of strength, disorder, and the supernatural." The material for his teaching was derived chiefly from the classics, four ancient books which he himself compiled and edited—comprising a volume of history, one of poetry, one of divination, and one of rules of propriety—together with a fifth book of his own composition, *Spring and Autumn*. With these Five Classics a sixth, devoted to the virtue of filial piety, is sometimes included. Confucius spoke daily on the classics and regarded them as indispensable for the formation of character. His educational programme was to arouse first an interest in the poets, then establish character by the study of manners and customs, and finish with music. So convinced was he of the formative influence of these books that he said, "When you enter any state you can know what its people have been taught," and he elaborated the statement by enumerating not only the particular virtues inculcated by the study of each of the classics but also the failings brought about by too exclusive attention to any one of them.

Evidently both religion and education were valued by Confucius primarily as means to the end of forming character. This is equally true of government. The fact that he devoted himself so largely to practical administration and the counselling of rulers is enough to show how important good government was in Confucius' eyes, but the chief end of government was always the promotion of virtue among the people. Consequently the most necessary qualification for governing was good conduct on the part of the ruler himself. "If a man can make his own conduct correct, what difficulty will he have in governing others? If he cannot, how can he govern others?" A good example is the best government. "To govern is to rectify. If you lead on the people with correctness, who will dare not to be correct?" The example of the ruler is the most effective deterrent of crime: "if the ruler were not covetous, the people would not rob, even though you should hire them to do it." Hence capital punishment is futile and unnecessary: "Why should you kill at all? Let your shown desires be for what is good, and the people will be good." If the people do not respect their ruler, good government is impossible. "The requisites of government are that there should be sufficiency of food, sufficiency of military equipment, and the confidence of the people in their ruler. If you have to give up one of the three, give up military equipment first; if two of the three, give up equipment and food, but keep the confidence of the people."

The type of character which Confucius desired to establish by government, education, and religion is expressed in the ideal of "the superior man." He who merits this designation does not seek riches or fame: "Coarse rice for food, water for drink, and one's bended arm for a pillow, even in the midst of these there is happiness; but riches and honors gained by injustice are to me light as the fleeting cloud." Virtue is more important than success: "Be not vexed that you have not a government appointment, but be anxious to possess the requisite qualifications; be not grieved that you are not known, but seek to be worthy of being known." The superior man is modest, reverent, sincere, and self-possessed. His conduct is governed by reason. "The man of superior virtue bends his undivided attention to fundamental principles. Once established in these, virtuous practice naturally follows." Not all men are capable of so acting on the basis of reason: "You may cause the people to practise what is proper, but you cannot make them understand the grounds of their duty." Hence formal rules are necessary. Even the superior man, who knows the reasons underlying social conventions, needs the constant guidance of the rules. "If one had not the ceremonial rules, he would not know how to dispose of his hands and feet, or how to apply his ears and eyes; and his advancing and retiring, his bowings and giving place would be without any definite rules." Nothing, it would seem, could be more abhorrent to Confucius than unthinking obedience to a spontaneous impulse, however noble. Yet polished propriety is not the whole duty of man. "When a man's natural, honest plainness exceeds his ornamental accomplishments, he is a mere rustic; when his ornamental accomplishments exceed his natural, honest plainness, he is a scribe (or fop); but when substantial plainness and polite accomplishments are properly blended, they form a superior man."

One reason for the emphasis put upon social propriety is the fact that Confucius was not concerned with the happiness or perfection of the individual but with the welfare of the people as a whole. Character as he conceived it was a matter of social attitudes and relationships, and the essence of morality was the harmonious adjustment of these relationships. The superior man is above all the man who fits into his place in society and conducts himself properly in his relations with his fellow men. The Confucian ideal is commonly expressed in terms of the Five Relationships, *viz.*, "the relations of ruler and subject, father and son, husband and wife, elder brother and younger, friend and friend." The principle which governs these relationships is what Christians know as the Golden Rule. When asked for a single word to serve as a comprehensive rule of conduct Confucius gave the word, "reciprocity," defining it by the precept, "Do not do to others what you do not wish them to do to you." The ruler must govern as he would wish to be governed. The father must treat his son as he would wish to be treated by his own father, and the son must respect his father as he would wish to be respected by his own son. Filial piety is the most fundamental of all the virtues.

All of the Five Relationships but the last, it should be observed, are relations of subordination. Confucian reciprocity does not involve equality. At the same time, each relationship imposes obligations upon the superior as well as the inferior member. Toward every other person, high or low, one should conduct himself with due respect. "The superior man's respect is universal. Wherein it appears the greatest is in his respect for himself. He is a branch from his parents. If he is not able to respect his own person, he is wounding his parents. If he wounds his parents, he wounds his own root; and when the root is wounded, the branches will follow it in its dying. These three things apply to the body politic. One's own person reaches to the persons of others; one's own son to the sons of others; one's own wife to the wives of others. If a ruler do these things his conduct will reach to all under the sky and all the states and families will be docilely obedient."

Not only respect should be cultivated but benevolence, which is defined as love for all men. This principle, however, is not carried to the point of unthinking self-sacrifice. Someone asked Confucius, "If a man of perfect virtue be told that a person has fallen into a well, must he descend and save him?" "Why should he?" replied the sage. "A superior man will do his utmost but will not throw away his life. He may be imposed upon by what has the appearance of reason, but not by what is plainly unreasonable." Nor did Confucius accept Lao-tze's principle of rewarding good for evil. When asked about it he said, "With what, then, will you requite kindness? Requite injury with justice, and kindness with kindness." Quite consistently, therefore, he sanctioned the practice of blood-revenge.

Like Lao-tze, Confucius did not in any strict sense originate a new religion. Lao-tze expounded a mystical philosophy from which an organized religion was later developed; Confucius strengthened and perpetuated the established national religion as a part of the social order to whose preservation his life was devoted. His influence has been, as he intended, conservative, but it has not been for that reason less important. Few men have ever moulded the life of a great people as he has. Confucianism is both a religion and a social system. As a religion it is one of several accepted by the Chinese people; as a social system it has dominated the life of the whole nation.

Chapter Four

MAHAVIRA

ASCETIC AND ATHEIST

Leaving China, where we have sat at the feet of Lao-tze and Confucius, we now cross the Himalayas into India to learn of Mahavira, the atheist who has become a god. In order to understand Mahavira and his teaching we must first acquaint ourselves with some of the chief facts about religion in India in his day. Then, as now, the most outstanding feature of the whole life of India was the caste system. At the top of the social ladder stood the priestly class, the Brahmans; next below were the Kshatriyas, the warriors and rulers; below these were the artisans; and at the bottom stood the Sudras, or serfs. Each of these four main castes, of course, has been subdivided into many minor divisions, but the fact of chief importance for us now is that the highest caste was that of the priests.

The religion of which these Brahmans were the official representatives involved an elaborate system of rites, so potent that the gods were practically at the beck and call of the Brahman priesthood. The other castes, consequently, were dependent upon the Brahmans for salvation. Only by the priestly rites could they have any hope of happiness either in this life or in the hereafter. At the same time among the Brahmans themselves there had come to be much dissatisfaction with this religion of salvation by ritual. Having made the gods their servants, they ceased to fear or to respect them and sought a higher Power. They were dissatisfied also with the earlier belief in a heaven for the good and a hell for the wicked. Another conception of the future life had arisen to haunt their thoughts, and it has continued to haunt the thought of India down to the present day. This was the conception of the transmigration of the soul. Before the time of Mahavira this belief had come to play a controlling part in the religious hopes and fears of India.

Now the prospect of repeated reincarnations may be a pleasant one if you believe that life is worth living over and over again. Modern theosophy holds out the hope of reincarnation as Christianity holds out the hope of heaven. But it was not so for ancient India. The Brahman doctrine of transmigration was colored by a thoroughgoing pessimism with regard to the value and desirability of living. Perhaps this life would look less attractive and precious to us if we believed that we should have to repeat it through endless cycles of ages, especially if we lived in the enervating climate of India and under the hard conditions of Indian life. For the Brahman thinkers the thought of the ceaseless circle of rebirth was a thought of terror; they could think of nothing more to be desired than release from the chain of reincarnation. Salvation therefore came to mean to them, not the attainment of heaven, which could only be a temporary way-station between incarnations, but release from the awful necessity of coming back at all. If only one could find a way to escape from life altogether and forever, that would be salvation indeed.

How can such emancipation be achieved? What is the law which governs the series of rebirths? According to Brahman thought it is the law of the Deed (Karma).

Every act, every thought, every desire of our hearts is a link in an eternal chain of cause and effect. The life we are now living is what it is because of our deeds in previous incarnations, and what we are doing now is determining in what form we shall come back to earth the next time, and whether we shall go through heaven or hell, or perhaps several heavens or hells, before we return to earth. We are bound by the Karma we have accumulated in other lives, and we are acquiring Karma which will bind us in the future. The secret of salvation, therefore, lies in discovering a way to escape or throw off our Karma. This secret the Brahmans believed they had found, and their idea of it leads into the very heart of their philosophy. For they were philosophers—at any rate there were philosophers among them. They had developed some of the most profound metaphysical conceptions the mind of man has ever framed, and they had done this long before the birth of philosophy among the Greeks. In Mahavira's time Greek philosophy was just leaving its cradle and learning to crawl; Socrates and Plato came a full century later.

The central idea of the Brahman philosophy is monism, the view that all reality is One. This means that all distinctions and differences, all change and motion, all diversity and multiplicity of any sort are only apparent. There seem to be different objects, different qualities, different persons in the world, but they have no real independent existence. There is only one reality, and it is unchanging, undivided, undistinguished, without parts or qualities. The name given by the ancient thinkers of India to this sole reality was Brahman; it was called Atman, or Self, because it is the real universe, as my self is the real "me." Sometimes Brahman-Atman is spoken of as a sort of World-Soul, as God, but the conception is essentially impersonal rather than personal. Brahman is the universe and the universe is Brahman; everything in the world is Brahman, or else it is unreal. You and I have no real existence as separate beings. In so far as we are real at all, we are Brahman. "That, O Soul, art thou," is the overwhelming thought in which the whole philosophy culminates.

According to Brahman thought, when one has truly grasped this great truth of truths he realizes that all this living and dying and living again is nothing but a part of the world-illusion, the mirage of distinctions and changes which obscures the oneness of reality. Consequently when one comes to the perception that he is Brahman, the veil drops from his eyes; he is free; his soul is absorbed in the universal sea of pure being; "there is no returning." Salvation is no longer achieved by ritual but by knowledge, the knowledge that we and Brahman are one. Such emancipating knowledge is not to be acquired by study. It does not come from books or from hearsay. It cannot be taught. It can come only as a direct, immediate perception; it must be seen. It is the knowledge of the mystic's vision. Only by this beatific spiritual vision, by personal spiritual experience, can release from Karma and reincarnation be found.

Not all the thinkers of India accepted this monistic mysticism. There were some philosophers who held that reality is twofold: matter and spirit, they said, are distinct and different. These dualistic philosophers also, however, adopted the conception of salvation by mystical experience. Karma and transmigration, they held, belong to the connection between the soul and the material world; there-

fore salvation is achieved, not by the knowledge that you
are Brahman, but by the knowledge that you are not matter—you are spirit, and it is your entanglement with the
world of matter which is illusory and unreal.

All this, of course, was far above the heads of the common people. For them the priests continued to carry on the
ancient system of sacrifices and prayers to the old gods and
to teach the hope of heaven and the fear of hell. But for
those of deeper spirituality the supreme quest of life was the
quest of mystical vision and complete emancipation from
the cycle of rebirths. Methods of physical and intellectual
discipline were devised for cultivating the trance-state, in
which the saving vision was achieved. Deliverance was
sought also by the practice of asceticism, the renunciation
of all pleasure and comfort and the reduction of life to the
barest and hardest necessities. India more than any other
country honors the man who denies and punishes himself.
The popular Indian idea of holiness is not so much serving
others as torturing oneself. For some asceticism is a way
of attaining mystic vision; for others it simply acquires
merit, a sort of celestial credit on the cosmic ledger; to
still others it means avoiding action which produces Karma,
and so gradually wearing out the Karma of previous incarnations until one is able to attain complete release.

Such were the dominant religious conceptions of India in
the days when Mahavira lived. The caste system, with the
Brahmans at the top, the system of sacrificial rites, the ideas
of transmigration and Karma and the awful significance
given to them by the pessimism of Indian thought, the
monistic doctrine of Brahman-Atman as the one and only
reality, the way of salvation by mystical knowledge, and

the practice of asceticism—these form the background of the life and teaching of Mahavira, which apart from them would be quite incomprehensible.

Like Lao-tze, Mahavira was born near the beginning of the sixth century B.C. and lived through the greater part of that century. When Lao-tze was teaching his disciples the mystery of the Tao in China, Mahavira in India was founding the religion known as Jainism. Like Lao-tze, also, and unlike Confucius, Mahavira is believed by his followers to have been of supernatural origin. According to the scriptures of Jainism, he was the last of a long series of divine saviors, or Tirthankaras, who had appeared through the ages. Some of these had lived in the remote periods of antiquity. They had enjoyed a length of life beside which the hundreds of years attributed to the early patriarchs in Genesis are like the life of an insect. They had also been of great stature: the earliest was five hundred bow-shots tall, but each succeeding Tirthankara was fifty bow-shots shorter than his predecessor, so that Mahavira had only normal human dimensions. Before his birth as a divine deliverer he had been incarnate many times and had lived for many ages among the gods on high. When the time came for his advent, he descended to earth and was born as the child of a rajah in the northeastern part of India. He was not his father's first child, for an older brother and sister are referred to in the Jain books.

But the most marvellous part of the story has not yet been told. Mahavira enjoys the unique distinction among the founders of religions, if not among all the sons of men, of having had two mothers. Being of royal blood, he belonged of course to the warrior caste, but he had narrowly escaped being born as a Brahman, which from the point of view of Jainism would have been a great misfortune. The story of his birth clearly reflects the fact that Jainism was a revolt against the social and religious domination of the priestly caste. In a previous incarnation, it seems, Mahavira had heard that he was to be a Tirthankara, and this knowledge had so filled him with pride that he had accumulated much Karma, with the result that he was nearly reborn as a member of the priestly class. Indeed when he descended from heaven he actually entered the womb of a Brahman woman. On the night when this occurred, she who was so blessed had fourteen "illustrious, beautiful, lucky, blest, auspicious, fortunate, great dreams." Awaking, "glad, pleased, and joyful in mind," she arose and "neither hasty nor trembling, with a quick and even gait," went to her husband and told him her dreams. Equally "pleased, glad, joyful," he "grasped the meaning of those dreams with his own innate intellect and intuition" and thus described the son they were to have: "O beloved of the gods, . . . you will give birth to a lovely and handsome boy with tender hands and feet, with a body containing the entire and complete five organs of sense, with the lucky signs, marks, and good qualities; a boy of whose body all limbs will be well formed, and of full volume, weight, and length, of lovely figure like that of the moon! And this boy, after having passed his childhood, and with just ripened intellect, having reached the state of youth, will repeat, fully understand, and well retain in his mind the four Vedas: . . . he will be versed in the philosophy of the six categories, and well grounded in arithmetic, in phonetics, ceremonial, grammar, metre, etymology, and astronomy, and in many other brahmanical sciences besides." After all this it is not surprising to read that the prospective father "repeatedly expressed his extreme satisfaction."

Having received the interpretation of her dreams, the lady arose from her chair of state and went back to bed, but remained awake in order to guard her dreams by hearing "good, auspicious, pious, agreeable stories about gods and religious men." But for all these auspicious portents, the pious Brahman and his wife were doomed to disappointment. It could not be that so great a savior should be born as a Brahman; to prevent such a catastrophe the chief of the gods came down and transferred the embryo to the womb of a woman of the warrior caste. The same story of the fourteen wonderful dreams is now repeated, but in this case the husband consults the interpreters of dreams regarding the meaning of his wife's remarkable visions. The account recalls the story of Daniel and his interpretation of the dream of Nebuchadnezzar, though the simplicity of the biblical narrative is in strong contrast to the elaboration and exasperating repetition of the Indian books. The king's dressing, exercising, and bathing before his conference with the interpreters of dreams are all related in minute detail.

Even before he was born Mahavira was remarkably considerate: he lay perfectly still, until his mother thought he was dead, and the court was plunged in grief; then, realizing what had happened, he "quivered a little" to allay their misapprehension. He received the most thorough prenatal care, and in due time "Trisali, perfectly healthy herself, gave birth to a perfectly healthy boy, the Venerable Ascetic Mahavira." A "godly lustre" made by "ascending and descending gods and goddesses" attended his birth.

The gods "rained down a shower of nectar, sandal powder, gold, and pearls" and anointed the child as a Tirthankara. Meanwhile, as a consequence of their divine visitation, the family had increased in worldly wealth, much of which they distributed to others. When Mahavira was born they made a great celebration: prisoners were released, fines and taxes remitted, debts cancelled, and plays and dances were given for ten days.

No pains were spared to give the child the care suited to his royal lineage. He had five nurses—a wet nurse, a nurse to clean him, one to dress him, one to play with him, and one to carry him. When he passed from childhood into maturity, he enjoyed all "the allowed, noble, fivefold joys and pleasures, consisting in sound, touch, taste, color, and smell." He married, and the scriptures tell of a daughter and a granddaughter. Thus until about the age of thirty Mahavira led the normal life of an Indian prince, remaining with his parents as long as they lived. When they died, however, and his elder brother became the ruler of the little kingdom, Mahavira began to give away his gold and silver, his troops and chariots, and other treasures. He had decided to devote himself to the spiritual life. With the consent of his brother, "tearing out his hair, he left the house, and entered the state of homelessness," paying "obeisance to all liberated spirits," and vowing "to do no sinful act." At that moment, we are told, "the whole assembly of men and gods stood motionless, like the figures on a picture."

Having "adopted the holy conduct," Mahavira at once "reached the knowledge by which he knew the thought of all sentient beings." He resolved to neglect his body for twelve years and to suffer with equanimity "all calamities arising from divine powers, men, or animals." Thus, meditating "on his Self, in blameless lodgings, in restraint, kindness, avoidance of sinful influence, chaste life, in patience, freedom from passion, contentment, . . . practising religious postures and acts," he "endured, sustained, and suffered all calamities." For a year and a month he wore clothes; thereafter he discarded even this concession to the flesh. Often "many sorts of living beings gathered on his body, crawled about it and caused pain there." Once, as he sat immovable in a religious posture, some cruel villagers cut his flesh, tore his hair, covered him with dust, and tossed him into the air and let him fall. Again one day he was sitting in meditation, when a group of rustics kindled a fire between his feet and even went so far as to drive nails into his ears, but Mahavira was quite unconscious of it all. At still another time he sat down to meditate according to his wont, crossing his ankles and gazing at the tip of his nose until he became absorbed. A passing farmer asked the ascetic to watch his bullocks for a while, but Mahavira did not even see him. When the farmer returned the bullocks had disappeared, but while he was looking for them they came back and lay down beside Mahavira. Finding them there in the morning, after searching all night, the farmer accused Mahavira of trying to steal them and began to beat him, but the god Indra intervened. Mahavira would not allow Indra to guard him from further molestation, but the god induced the saint's cousin to protect him without letting him know it.

So the twelve years were spent, as Mahavira had resolved. Finally, in the thirteenth year, as he sat on the bank of a river "in a squatting position, with heels joined, exposing himself to the heat of the sun, with the knees high and the head low, in deep meditation, he reached Nirvana, the complete and full, the unobstructed, unimpeded, infinite and supreme best knowledge and intuition called Kevala." He was now a Jain, or Conqueror, and "knew all conditions of the world, of men, gods, and demons, whence they come, where they go, whether they are born as men or animals, or become gods or hell-beings, their food, drink, desires, conversation and gossip, and the thoughts of their minds." From now on he devoted himself to teaching and to the organization of a monastic order. During the remaining thirty years of his life he travelled about from place to place, remaining in no village, except in the rainy season, for more than one night. When he spoke, we are told, he was understood by all creatures, whatever their language. Four kings heard him and gave their approval to his teaching. According to Jacobi, a leading authority on Jainism, Mahavira's high family connections were of great use to him in promoting his order. Eleven chief disciples are named in the books, but only one of them outlived his master and carried on the work.

One day when Mahavira was seventy-two years old, having worn out all his Karma, he sat in the "office of the writers" of a certain ruler, "reciting the fifty-five lectures which detail the results of Karma; and the thirty-six unasked questions." He had "just explained the chief lecture" when he "cut asunder the ties of birth, old age, and death" and was "finally liberated, freed from all pains." His death, like his birth, was attended by gods and goddesses. That night his oldest disciple attained perfect knowledge by severing the tie of personal friendship for his master. That night also eighteen kings held a great "illumination," saying, "Since the light of intelligence is gone, let us make an illumination of material matter."

It will be remembered that Mahavira is regarded by his followers as only one of a series of saviors. The one who preceded him in the series, and who is believed to have lived two hundred and fifty years before his time, was in all probability a historical person and the founder of a sect of which Mahavira's parents were members. Mahavira was undoubtedly much influenced by this earlier sect; in fact the chief difference between its teaching and his seems to be that to the four vows required of its members he added the vow of chastity. Another teacher who seems to have influenced him was an ascetic named Gosala, with whom he lived for six years. Mahavira may have derived from Gosala the rule forbidding clothing. Perhaps, as Jacobi suggests, Mahavira endeavored to combine Gosala's order with the earlier sect which has been mentioned. At any rate he eventually parted from Gosala and founded an independent order. The Jainas claim that Gosala, for all his asceticism, was unchaste; if so, this may have been the reason for the separation and for Mahavira's adding the vow of chastity to the vows of the earlier order.

The teaching of Mahavira is summed up in "The Three Jewels"—right faith, right knowledge, and right conduct. Right faith means simply belief in Mahavira as the Conqueror (Jain), who has found and revealed the true way of salvation. Right knowledge means the knowledge of his philosophical teachings. Mahavira rejected the conception of Brahman-Atman as the sole reality and accepted the dualistic conception of the universe as consisting of matter and an infinite number of souls. He also denied that there was any god who could save mankind. "Man!" he said, "Thou art thy own friend! Why wishest thou for a friend beyond thyself?" Consequently not only the old system of sacrifices but prayer, at least in the sense of petition for help from any superhuman power, is utterly condemned by Jainism. Even an anxious mother's prayer for the recovery of a sick child is regarded as sinful. Prayer is practised by the Jainas only in the form of adoration of the twenty-four Tirthankaras.

With regard to the hereafter Mahavira's teaching was not so revolutionary. He retained the doctrines of transmigration and Karma; in fact they lie at the root of the whole system, for Jainism, like most of the religions of India, is essentially a way of deliverance from the fear of rebirth. Mahavira's conception of Karma, however, differed somewhat from that of the other religions of India. He pictured Karma as a sort of material coating accumulated by the soul in successive layers as the result of its deeds. The way to avoid rebirth was to wear away these layers of Karma by the strictest asceticism. When the soul has accomplished this, according to the Jain scriptures, it "takes the form of a straight line, goes in one moment, without touching anything, and taking no space, upwards to the highest Akasa, and there develops into its natural form, obtains perfection, enlightenment, deliverance, and final beatitude." The favorite term for this blessed state among the Jainas is Moksha, deliverance. It is also called Nirvana, extinction, as in Buddhism, but the Jainas deny that Nirvana means the annihilation of the soul. Moksha, they say, is not nothingness nor absorption but "a state of being without qualities, emotions, or relations, and removed from the possibility of rebirth." The difference between nothingness and a state without qualities or relations, it must be confessed, is rather obscure to a Western mind. For those who have not attained Moksha there is a series of heavens, and for the wicked a series of hells. The descriptions given in the scriptures of the various places and kinds of torment remind the Christian reader of Dante.

With right faith and right knowledge goes the third of "The Three Jewels," right conduct. The Jainas take pride in the fact that their religion brings practical ethics and philosophical speculation together. The Jaina philosophy evinces remarkable psychological and moral insight. This may be illustrated by the story of Kapila, a poor orphan who was sent by his friends to beg at the court of a king noted for his liberality. Upon being offered the two coins which the king was accustomed to give all beggars, Kapila said that they were not enough to relieve his extreme poverty. The wise king told him to make up his mind how much it would take to satisfy him. The attempt to do so brought Kapila to the realization that he would still be unsatisfied if he had half the kingdom. Alarmed at the thought of all the Karma which such greed would incur, he devoted himself to the ascetic's life of complete self-denial as his only hope of escape.

In considering Mahavira's ethical teaching, we must distinguish between the vows required of the monks and the standards of conduct for laymen. Mahavira not only organized a monastic order but a community of lay adherents also. This is one of the outstanding differences between

Jainism and Buddhism; it is also one of the secrets of the survival of Jainism, for monasticism is socially parasitic, depending upon the support of more worldly-minded laymen. Only a monk, to be sure, can hope to attain deliverance from rebirth. The layman's highest hope is that in his next incarnation he may be good enough to become a monk. Even a nun—for there are Jain nuns as well as monks—can expect no more. To be born as a woman is in itself enough to show that one has not attained the last incarnation.

Like Mahavira himself, the monk must practise the strictest asceticism, in order to wear out the Karma of previous incarnations and stop the acquisition of further Karma. With rare consistency Jainism holds that the ultimate step in this process is self-starvation, but of course this is only for the saint who has taken all the previous steps and reached the threshold of Nirvana. No discomfort is too great for the Jain monk: heat and cold must be endured without even wishing for the comfort of a bath or a fire. Insects must not be brushed away nor annoyance felt if they sting. Twenty-two troubles which the monk must conquer are enumerated, including women as well as insects, kind as well as abusive treatment, understanding as well as ignorance, and, last of all, righteousness—though why some of these are regarded as "troubles" is not altogether clear.

Five vows are taken by the monk. The first is that he will not take life in any form. The doctrine of non-injury (ahimsa) is pushed to the utmost extreme in Jainism. To avoid treading upon insects the monk carries a brush and carefully sweeps the path before him. Only boiled water may be used for drinking or washing, and someone else must do the boiling. Of course no flesh may be eaten. The monk's diet, indeed, is very limited, for many forms of vegetable life are included under this vow. They too, according to Jain belief, have souls: potatoes, beets, and the like have not one soul but many. The second of the five vows requires the avoidance of all forms of dishonesty, and the third renounces "all taking of anything not given." The Jainas, laity as well as monks, are noted for their high standard of honesty. A man who cheats is threatened with rebirth as a woman.

The fourth vow is that of chastity, which is much emphasized. This is the vow, the reader will remember, which Mahavira himself added to the requirements of the earlier order of which he and his parents had been members. For the monk, of course, chastity means celibacy. One of the sacred books of Jainism gives a forbidding picture of the fate of a monk who breaks his vow and marries. He must fetch and carry for his wife, bring her lip-salve, ribbons, combs, and looking-glasses, and hold the baby or hand it to its mother. "Thus some supporters of their sons have to carry burdens like camels. Getting up in the night they lull the baby asleep like nurses. . . . This has been done by many men who for the sake of pleasures have stooped so low; they become the equals of slaves, animals, servants, beasts of burden—mere nobodies." Yet, as marriage is regulated by Jain law, the husband's lot is not altogether unattractive: his wife must prepare his meals and eat only when he has finished, "and in the evening, when the husband comes home tired, she massages him."

The fifth and last vow requires the severing of all personal attachments. Even devotion to Mahavira himself is forbidden. His chief disciple found this requirement an obstacle to his spiritual progress until the very night of Mahavira's death: only then was he able to stop saying "*my* master" and so enter into perfect knowledge.

Such a complete eradication of all natural feelings is not expected of the layman. The ideal held before him is, on the whole, that of normal social living on a high moral plane. As the early Catholic Church specified seven deadly sins, so Jainism especially condemns seven kinds of wrong-doing: "gambling, eating meat, wine-bibbing, adultery, hunting, thieving, debauchery." In the avoidance of alcohol the Jains are so strict that they avoid even the use of European medicines. The life of a sinner is thus described in the Jain scriptures: "An ignorant man kills, lies, deceives, calumniates, dissembles, drinks liquor, and eats meat, thinking that this is right. Overbearing in acts and words, desirous for wealth and women, he accumulates sins. . . . Then he suffers ill, and is attacked by disease, and is in dread of the next world, when he reflects on his deeds." The ideal also has its positive side. The twenty-one qualities of a Jain gentleman are enumerated as follows: "He will always be serious in demeanor; clean as regards both his clothes and his person; good-tempered; striving after popularity; merciful; afraid of sinning; straightforward; wise; modest; kind; moderate; gentle; careful in speech; sociable; cautious; studious; reverent both to old age and old customs; humble; grateful; benevolent; and, finally, attentive to business."

While the life of the Jain layman is thus, from our point of view, much more normal than that of the monk, still the fundamental ideal of asceticism produces a puritanical suspicion of everything pleasant and enjoyable. The Jain young people of to-day, it is said, are becoming discontented with this ascetic standard, feeling "that the ideal needed for modern life is the development, not the negation, of personality." The fact that doing nothing is more laudable than doing good is also held responsible for a certain lack of public spirit and social-mindedness among the Jainas. Lao-tze's doctrine of doing nothing will be recalled in this connection, but Lao-tze was not an ascetic. A life of simple non-striving was his ideal, not the strenuous conquest and suppression of self demanded by Mahavira.

Credit must be given Mahavira for one great advance in social ideals: he rejected the caste system. Unfortunately, however, like many other features of the popular religion which he condemned, the observance of caste distinctions has crept back into Jainism. While we are bound to regret this relapse to a lower ideal, we who call ourselves Christians are not in a position to throw the first stone. It is also to be regretted that the high ideals of Jainism are limited in their practical working by the primitive conception of ritual uncleanness or tabu. There are thirty-two conditions, for example, which make it unlawful to read the scriptures, though in the absence of such conditions it is the duty of the Jain layman to read the scriptures every day!

Not only caste distinctions, but practical polytheism and idolatry have crept back into Jainism. Temples have been built for worship, and the ritual is committed to Brahman priests, who do not have to believe in Jainism but are qualified by their caste-standing for the sacred office. The Tirthankaras, including Mahavira himself, are venerated as divine beings. They are not, however, resorted to for material or spiritual blessings, but are adored as models of perfection. For practical assistance the Jainas turn rather to the gods of their Hindu neighbors. Perhaps the greatest departure from the spirit of Mahavira's teaching is the change from a universal, missionary religion, a way of salvation for all men, to one that is purely hereditary. The original spirit of evangelism did not persist; Jainism has never spread beyond the bounds of India and is now declining. Its adherents number only about one million.

As the preliminary reflections of our introduction might lead one to expect, Mahavira was preceded by other men whose work he only carried on, with some additions of his own. His followers also have continued to modify the religion, though chiefly by resuming earlier beliefs and practices which he discarded. Nevertheless he was, more truly than either Lao-tze or Confucius, the creator of the religion which regards him as its founder. He not only formulated the doctrines which it still (officially, at least) maintains, but also gave it its distinctive form of organization. Not without reason is the name of the religion derived from the Jain, the Conqueror, who overcame the world and self without recourse to any god or savior. We may or may not agree with the statement of Professor Hopkins that a religion which denies God, worships man, and nourishes vermin has no right to exist, but we cannot fairly withhold our admiration for the moral earnestness and strength of will displayed by Mahavira and his most faithful followers.

CHAPTER FIVE

BUDDHA

COMPASSIONATE RATIONALIST

HE who by virtue of his spiritual experience and insight is known the world over as the Buddha, the Enlightened, belonged to the Sakya clan of northern India and is therefore often called Sakyamuni, the Sage of the Sakyas. His family name was Gautama and his given name Siddharta. Like Mahavira he was a prince of the warrior caste. Born about 560 B.C., he was about forty years younger than Mahavira, and the span of his life coincided almost exactly with that of Confucius.

His followers differ somewhat among themselves regarding his origin and nature. All agree, of course, that he had often been incarnate before, but the Buddhists of Tibet, China, and Japan regard him as one of a great company of divine beings, while those of southern lands hold that he was not a god but only a great teacher, though a most marvellous one. Sometimes it is gravely stated that he was not over sixteen feet tall: images of him are often of that height, but it is hard to say whether the tradition is based on the height of the images or *vice versa*. However that may be, there can be no doubt as to the Buddha's spiritual stature. In character, in life, and in intellect there are few indeed who can be compared with him. What Jesus said of John the Baptist we can well imagine he would have said of Gautama: "Among them that are born of women there hath not arisen a greater." Different as were their environments, and profound as are some of the differences in their teachings, none of the founders of the other religions was so much like Jesus as was "the Light of Asia."

Like Mahavira he is believed to have descended from heaven to become incarnate. His birth was not otherwise miraculous, except that he was born from his mother's right side without causing her pain. From all accounts he was a remarkable baby. No sooner was he born than he took seven steps and announced his mission in a voice like that of a bull. Peculiar physical marks attested his superiority to other men. He had a thousand-rayed wheel on the soles of his feet, a web-like filament between his fingers, and a tuft like white wool between his eyes. His mother died when he was only a week old, and he was nursed by an aunt, who many years later became the first Buddhist nun.

Even in childhood the boy's mind displayed a serious bent. "His bodily frame was small, but his heart was established, not disturbed by glittering baubles." Stories are told, as in the case of other founders of religions, of his excelling his teachers. His father seems to have been disturbed by the boy's lack of interest in the usual pursuits of a prince. Everything that could be done to wean him from morbid reflection was done, but in vain. When he reached the proper age, his father found him a lovely bride "to allure by pleasant wiles his heart" from serious matters. Buddhist writers picture her as one of the most attractive heroines of the world's literature, "majestic as a queen of heaven, constant ever, cheerful night and day, full of dignity and exceeding grace." When she gave birth to a little boy, the delighted grandfather felt sure that his son would no longer be inclined to leave home and become an ascetic. But the additional domestic tie only made Siddharta feel more keenly the necessity of escaping from earthly bonds.

He was overwhelmed by the universal and essential misery of life. Professor G. F. Moore, speaking of the fact that most of Buddha's early followers came from the upper classes, makes a statement which is worth pondering in connection with the experience of Gautama himself: "It is a common observation that it is not the people whose life seems to us most intolerable that are most discontented with life; despair is a child of the imagination, and pessimism has always been a disease of the well-to-do or at least the comfortably-off, and peculiarly virulent when it attacks youth." The young Sakya prince had, as we should say, everything that money could buy, but he was profoundly unhappy, and it is all to his credit that it was the misery of others which made him so. Like the Prophet of Nazareth, "when he saw the multitudes he was moved with compassion for them."

The experience which finally led him to his Great Renunciation is presented in a story which is doubtless unhistorical, as regards details, but is significant psychologically. Once while riding in his chariot Siddharta saw an old man and was horrified by the ravages which time had made. His father's efforts to keep from him everything that might arouse unwholesome brooding only made this unwonted sight more terrible. In like manner he encountered one day the loathsome spectacle of disease, and on a third

occasion, meeting a funeral procession, he beheld the end
to which all men must come. Old age, disease, and death—
this, it seemed to him, was what life meant. From then on
his whole heart's desire was to find the way of escape from
all this suffering. "Sorrow I teach," he used to say in later
years, "sorrow and the eradication of sorrow." He was op-
pressed, to borrow the language of Wordsworth, by "the
heavy and the weary weight of all this unintelligible
world." Then one day he went out again and sat watching
some men plowing a field, and "his heart was moved with
piteous feeling to see the laborers struggling, bent bodies,
hair dishevelled, dripping with sweat, and fouled with
dirt." The plight of the patient oxen also aroused his sympathy. But as he reflected on the sight, a wandering ascetic
came that way. His untroubled mien and the light in his
eyes convinced the troubled prince that here at last was the
way of peace, and he resolved, regardless of the cost to himself and to those he loved, to leave his home and follow
the way of self-denial until he had found deliverance for
himself and all sentient beings.

Gautama was now twenty-nine years old. The crucial
point in his life had come. The uncertainty and struggle
were over; the "divided self" was "integrated"; he knew
what he must do and did not shrink from it. His father,
whom he informed of his resolution, pleaded with him
desperately, but without avail. His wife was not told what
he intended to do; for he wished to spare her as long as possible, and perhaps he also feared that her entreaties would
be more than he could stand. During the night, while she
lay sleeping with her babe at her side, he stole away, allowing himself only a lingering look by way of farewell,

and with his faithful charioteer and his great white horse went out into the dark. This Great Renunciation has been glorified in art and literature as the birth of Buddhism. And lest any one should think it strange that a great religion has grown out of a man's deserting his wife and child, be it here remembered that Another once said, "If any man cometh unto me and hateth not his own father, and mother, and wife, and children, and brethren, and sisters, yea, and his own life also, he cannot be my disciple." The same Teacher when told one day that his own mother and brothers were seeking him, said, "My mother and my brethren are these that know the word of God and do it."

Far from his home Siddharta rode before he dismounted and, exchanging clothes with a passing huntsman, sent back his charioteer with his horse and his princely jewels and walked on alone. His father, still unwilling to let him go, repeatedly sent court officials after him to induce him to return. Of course the writers of the ancient books which tell the story considered Gautama's action altogether right and holy, yet it is remarkable how forcibly they state the arguments used by the father's messengers. With true dramatic instinct the grief-stricken father's point of view is fairly presented; Gautama's case is so strong that it needs no artificial support in the telling. No argument can turn him from his sacred quest of deliverance. When the ties of kinship are urged as a reason for his return, he replies, "As men going along a road suddenly meet midway with others, and then in a moment more are separated, each going his own way, so by the force of concomitance relationships are framed, and then, according to each one's destiny, there is separation. In this world there is rupture of family love; in another life it is sought for again, brought together a moment, again rudely divided."

Six years of stern asceticism now followed. With two successive teachers Gautama studied the philosophy of the Brahman thinkers and the discipline they had devised for cultivating the mystic trance. Then, convinced that these did not reach the root of the matter, he withdrew and undertook an even more severe self-mortification, "each day eating only one hemp grain, his body shrunken, his heart of wisdom increasing more and more in light." Soon he became known through all the country round about. Five other ascetics joined him.

So far the story is not unlike that of Mahavira and many another Indian saint, but now comes the most remarkable part of all. Gautama had tried the way of the self-induced trance; he had tried the way of denying the flesh. Now, with amazing sanity and independence, he decided that all this was a mistake, and that what he needed was a bath and a meal! Forthwith he made his way to the nearby river. The water refreshed him, though he was so weak that he had to hold on to an overhanging branch to get out again. In this condition he was found by a herdsman's daughter, who gave him food. "All his members were refreshed, and he became capable of receiving Enlightenment." The five ascetics, however, believing that the flesh had proved stronger than the spirit, left him in disgust. Their point of view was that of the Jainas, who have caricatured Gautama's experience as follows: he was at first, they say, a Jain monk, but one day when he was sitting by the riverside he saw a dead fish float by and thought, since there was no soul in it, that there would be no harm in eating it; thus he was led to found a new religion. Certainly he had parted radically from the way of salvation taught by Mahavira.

But now came fierce temptation. According to the Buddhist scriptures, Death sent his daughters, Desire, Discontent, and Lust to tempt Gautama. Some accounts put this experience earlier in the story, but psychologically it is most likely that the first revulsion from asceticism would tend to carry him over to the opposite extreme, and that the returning strength of his body would bring back in full force the memory of the luxuries of his youth. At any rate the temptation was overcome, and now with "fixed mind at rest, thoroughly exhausting the first principles of truth, he entered into a deep and subtle contemplation." The mystic vision which he had hitherto sought in vain began to unfold at last. "During the first watch he entered on right perception, and in recollection all former births passed before his eyes." All night, through terror and doubt as well as hope and joy, his spirit mounted from one plane to another, until with the dawn came perfect light. The tree under which he was sitting has been known ever since as the Bo-tree, the tree of Enlightenment. Siddharta was now, at the age of thirty-five, the Buddha. The way of deliverance had been found.

Another temptation had now to be met. As the Buddha basked in the light, this thought occurred to him: "I have penetrated this doctrine which is profound, difficult to perceive and to understand, which brings quietude of heart, which is unattainable by reasoning, intelligible only to the wise. Why should I try to proclaim it to these people? If men are not able to understand my preaching there will

be weariness and annoyance for me." He could have passed
at once into Nirvana, but then mankind would have been
left to suffer as before. As the scriptures tell the story, the
god Brahma appeared to Buddha and said, "The Law
hitherto manifested has been impure; do thou now open
the door of the Immortal. Let them hear the doctrine of
the Spotless one." Three times he thus urged the needs of
the world. Then the Buddha, "full of compassion toward
sentient beings, looked over the world. He saw beings
whose mental eyes were darkened by scarcely any dust, and
beings whose eyes were covered with much dust, beings
sharp of sense and blunt of sense, of good disposition and
of bad disposition, easy to instruct and difficult to instruct,
some of them seeing the dangers of future life and of sin."
So "when he saw the multitudes, he was moved with compassion for them." He determined to proclaim deliverance
to mankind, and first of all, since his former teachers were
now dead, to the five ascetics with whom he had recently
practised self-denial. On the road, as he went to seek them,
he met a Brahman, to whom he announced his new-found
peace, but the Brahman shook his head, saying "It may be
so, friend," and went another way.

In the Deer Park at Benares Gautama found the five
ascetics. And now occurred one of the many touching incidents which eloquently bespeak his extraordinary personal
charm. The ascetics must have loved him, and what had
seemed to them his fall from grace must have been a bitter
disappointment to them, for as he approached they agreed
to ignore him, but "when he drew near them they kept
not their agreement. They went forth to meet the Blessed
One, took his bowl and robe, prepared a seat for him,

brought water for washing his feet, a footstool and a towel. They addressed him as 'Friend.' " Then he made known to them the salvation which he had found. "If you walk in the way I show you," he said, "you will ere long have penetrated to the truth, having yourselves known it and seen it face to face; and you will live in the possession of that highest goal of the holy life, for the sake of which noble youths fully give up the world and go forth into the houseless state." When they had heard his teaching, the five ascetics received it and became his disciples, and so the Buddhist order was inaugurated.

Other disciples gathered about him. One of the most noted incidents of this period in his life is the conversion of Yasa, a noble youth who had been most delicately nurtured. One night, apparently through sheer boredom, Yasa fell asleep in the midst of his female musicians. One by one the women also fell asleep. When Yasa awoke and saw them lying about in dishevelled and revolting postures, he arose in disgust and left the house. Without thinking where he was going, he walked about until he reached the Deer Park, where Buddha saw him and talked with him "about the merits obtained by alms-giving, about the duties of morality, about heaven, about the evils, the vanity, and the sinfulness of desires, and about the blessings of the abandonment of desire." When he had thus prepared the young man's mind, he taught him his cardinal doctrine of Suffering. Meanwhile Yasa's mother missed him and sent his father after him. Seeing the man coming, Buddha did not let him see his son at once but preached to him too, with the result that the father accepted the teaching and became Buddha's first lay-disciple. He was then permitted

to see Yasa and agreed to his ordination as a monk. After
that Buddha and Yasa took begging bowls and went together to Yasa's former home. Here the young man's
mother and wife asked for admittance to the order and
were received as the first female lay-disciples.

So many young noblemen adopted the religious life
under Gautama's direction that the people began to com-
plain. The Buddha, they said, was causing "fathers to be-
get no sons, wives to become widows, and families to become extinct." Undisturbed by the clamor, Gautama assured his disciples that it would last only a week, and when
the people saw that "it was by truth, and not by wrong"
that he led men, the opposition ceased. Many enemies and
dangers were overcome by the calm and fearless Enlightened One. Some murderers who had been sent against him
were converted. Once a wild elephant was let loose against
him, but it became gentle in his presence. It is even said
that a rock which was hurled at him from a precipice split
in two, and the pieces passed by him. Students of the New
Testament find especially interesting one instance of his
power given in the Buddhist scriptures. After a great rain
the place where he was staying was flooded, but he caused
the water to recede and walked up and down in the midst
of it on a spot covered with dust. One of his disciples went
out in a boat to look for him, and, when he saw him,
called to him, whereupon Buddha rose in the air and came
into the boat.

Not many months after the founding of his order, when
the number of his disciples had reached sixty, Gautama
called them together and sent them out to preach. From
then on he himself went about preaching during the eight

months when this was feasible, remaining in one place during the rainy season and teaching his disciples. His method of teaching was characterized by a gradual approach, giving each individual the truth as he was able to bear it. This principle is illustrated by a story which in some respects recalls the parable of the Prodigal Son, though its main import is quite different. The son of a certain householder went out to a far country and there wasted his substance until he began to be in want. His father meanwhile became very wealthy. Wandering about from place to place, the son came eventually to the place where his father was now living. Here he was recognized and summoned to his father's palace, but, thinking that he was about to be imprisoned by some local magnate, he fled. Recalled by his father's messengers, he was educated, given work, and gradually promoted as he demonstrated his worth. Only after many years, however, did the father make himself known. The moral of this tale is that "little by little must the minds of men be trained for higher truths."

An even closer parallel between a saying of Buddha and a passage in the New Testament may be noted here. As Paul, in the Epistle to the Ephesians, urges the Christian to put on "the whole armor of God," with "the breastplate of righteousness," "the shield of faith," "the helmet of salvation," and "the sword of the Spirit, which is the word of God," so Buddha, warning his disciples against women, said, "Take then the bow of earnest perseverance, and the sharp arrow-points of wisdom. Cover your head with the helmet of right thought."

One of the first places Gautama visited after sending

out his sixty disciples was his father's home. The story of
the meeting with his father, who had heard of his fame as
a teacher but was unprepared to see him as a wandering
beggar, is full of pathos, as is also the account of his meeting
with his wife, who since his departure had been living in
self-denial like his own. His son, Rahula, whom he had
left a baby, was now about eight years old. The boy's
mother, pointing out to him the Buddha, said, "This is
your father; go ask him for your inheritance." Rahula did
so and received as his inheritance ordination as a monk.
The method of ordaining a monk is told in this connection: the candidate was required to cut off his hair and
beard, put on a yellow robe and adjust it so as to cover one
shoulder, salute the feet of the monks with his head, sit
before them and raise his joined hands, and say three
times, "I take refuge in the Buddha, I take refuge in the
Law, I take refuge in the Order." Gautama's father asked
him to establish a rule that ordination should not be given
to young men without the consent of their fathers and
mothers: "For the love of a son, Lord," he said, "cuts into
the skin; having cut into the skin it cuts into the hide;
having cut into the hide it cuts into the flesh; having cut
into the flesh it cuts into the ligaments; having cut into the
ligaments it cuts into the bones; having reached the bones
it reaches the marrow and dwells in the marrow."

So far Gautama had not formed an order for women,
and he was reluctant to do so, though he received them as
lay-disciples. Three times his wife asked to be admitted to
the order but was refused. Then the aunt who had nursed
him in infancy came with his wife and other women, and
their entreaties were eloquently seconded by Ananda, Bud-

dhism's Beloved Disciple. Gautama could no longer refuse, but he told Ananda that the persistence of his religion in India would be shortened by five hundred years as the result of admitting women.

Like all monastic orders, that of Buddha was regulated by a set of rules, and many stories are told of the way in which they came to be imposed. Many of the rules thus attributed to Gautama himself were probably, as a matter of fact, developed gradually in response to situations which arose during the later history of the order. The stories ascribing them to Buddha grew out of the desire to give them the authority belonging to the founder's teaching. The same thing has happened sometimes in both the Old and New Testaments. Yet the stories at least reflect the fact that the rules were not promulgated all at once, but grew out of definite cases and precedents. For example, there were evidently some monks who came, as we should say, for the loaves and fishes. Such was the case of a young man named Upali, whose parents said, "If Upali learns writing, his fingers will become sore; if he learns arithmetic, his breast will become diseased; if he learns money-changing, his eyes will become sore; so we shall make of him a monk."

Unworthy motives like this necessitated more stringent rules of admission to the order. At one time the people of Magadha were so afflicted with the five diseases, "leprosy, boils, dry leprosy, consumption, and fits," that the doctors could not take care of all the sick. The Buddhist order, however, had a physician among its adherents, and the monks all received good medical treatment. Some of the people therefore decided to join the order, intending to return to the world when they got well. As a result Buddha had to make a rule denying admission to anyone afflicted with the five diseases. Soldiers also, reflecting that their occupation incurred much Karma, began to join the order in such numbers that their officers protested, and Buddha had to prohibit the ordination of any man in the royal service. The wearing of wooden shoes was forbidden because their clatter disturbed the brethren in their meditations; therefore the monks began to make shoes of palm and bamboo leaves, but this caused the plants to wither, and the people complained that the monks were destroying vegetable life. So Buddha had to forbid the use of the leaves.

Sometimes concessions and exceptions to the rules are justified by similar stories. The monks were forbidden to eat food not given to them, but once, it is said, some of them did not receive enough food from people along the way and went hungry, though there was abundance of fruit on the trees. Therefore Buddha decreed that if there was no one to give them the fruit, in such a case the monks might pick it, place it on the ground, then pick it up again and eat it.

Elaborate rules for the housekeeping of the monks were developed, though not necessarily in Buddha's own lifetime. In the scriptures they are given instructions for cleaning their rooms. First the alms bowl and robe are to be taken out, then the mat and sheet, pillow and mattress. The bed must be carried out without knocking it against the doorpost or rubbing it against the floor. Then the monk must remove the carpet and spread it out, sweep out all cobwebs, wipe clean the casements and the corners of the room, scour the walls, and mop and scour the floor. The carpet must be exposed to the sun, beaten, and replaced. Everything in the room is to be thoroughly sunned before it is put back.

In teaching and in the administration of the order the years were busily spent until Gautama was eighty years old. As our gospels tell more of the last week of Jesus' life than of all the previous years, so the account of Buddha's last days becomes more and more detailed as the end approaches. Many discourses with his disciples and with others are reported. The Buddha was now feeble and suffered much from sickness, yet he continued to teach and to go about from place to place. One day he was entertained by a smith named Chunda, who gave him the best he had, but the food was too rich for the worn-out constitution of the aged Buddha, and he was stricken with dysentery. Nevertheless he went on. Soon he had to stop and rest beneath a tree by the roadside, while the faithful Ananda brought him water and tried to make him comfortable. A man who came that way stopped and sat beside him, and in spite of his suffering the Buddha charmed the man with his high discourse. Then he did another thing which reveals his true nobility. He thought of Chunda, who had given him the fatal meal, and realizing how the poor man would feel, and how others might reproach him, he told Ananda to say to the smith that there were two offerings of food which brought special merit upon the giver, that given to a saint when he attained enlightenment and that given to him when he made his final escape from this life of sorrow.

Once more they went on until they came to a grove, where the Buddha lay down to die. Ananda voiced his grief that the disciples would now have no teacher, but Buddha said, "I am not the first Buddha who came upon earth, nor shall I be the last. I came to teach you the truth, and I have founded on earth the kingdom of truth. Gautama Siddharta will die, but Buddha will live, for Buddha is the truth, and the truth cannot die. He who believes in the truth and lives it is my disciple, and I shall teach him. The truth will be propagated, and the kingdom of truth will increase for about five hundred years. Then for a while the clouds of error will darken the light, and in due time another Buddha will arise, and he will reveal to you the selfsame eternal truth which I have taught."

"How shall we know him?" Ananda asked.

"The Buddha that will come after me," replied Gautama, "will be known as Maitreya, which means 'He whose name is kindness.'" The Buddhists still wait for Maitreya as the Jews still wait for their Messiah, but about five hundred years later than Gautama there came to earth one who, like him, was moved with compassion at the sorrow of men, and who not only was himself worthy to be called "His name is kindness," but also pointed beyond himself to a Father whose name is Love.

After this Buddha received many who wished to see him, and spoke with his disciples. His last words were "Dissolution is inherent in all composite things. With heedfulness work out your task." When he had said this he fell into deep meditation and having lost consciousness passed peacefully away.

Gautama was not only great in life and character; he was one of the world's greatest thinkers. His teaching displays the most remarkable intellectual power. His interest, it is true, was always practical rather than philosophical. After his Great Renunciation, when the ministers sent by his father tried to change his purpose by philosophical arguments, Gautama, "clear and unconfused, with no desire to wrangle after the way of the schools," replied, "The question of being or not being is an idle one, only adding to the uncertainty of the unstable mind. Purity of life, wisdom, the practice of asceticism—these are matters to which I earnestly apply myself. The world is full of empty studies." Like Confucius, Buddha avoided metaphysical questions. It may not be out of place to recall the fact that Jesus also answered a theoretical inquiry about the number of those who should be saved with the practical direction, "Strive to enter in at the strait gate." A consistent emphasis upon practical issues is no sign of intellectual weakness. The extraordinary keenness of Gautama's thinking will be evident as we examine his teaching.

With Mahavira, Buddha rejected the monistic conception of Brahman-Atman, the caste system (including the priestly claims of the Brahmans), and the ancient Vedic scriptures. For all practical purposes his teaching—again agreeing with that of Mahavira—is atheistic. The existence of the old gods is not denied, but they cannot help man to escape from the wheel of rebirth. Man must work out his own salvation, and there is no God that worketh in him either to will or to do.

In what he retained as well as in what he rejected of the older religious philosophy Gautama agreed with Mahavira. Transmigration, Karma, and the pessimistic view of life are as fundamental for Buddhism as for Jainism or Brahmanism. Yet we must qualify this statement, for transmigration and Karma do not mean in Buddhism what they mean in Jainism. Far from teaching, as Mahavira did, that the soul is eternal, Gautama taught that there is no such thing as a soul. Individual selfhood is the most basic and the most harmful of all our delusions. This does not mean that the soul is identical with the Absolute. Buddha differed from the Brahman philosophers as widely as he differed from Mahavira, for he denied a Self to the universe as well as to the individual. His argument is the exact opposite of that urged by the Greek philosopher Plato a century later. Plato said that the soul must be immortal, because dissolution means the separation of an object's component parts, and the soul has no parts to be separated. Gautama said that what we call the soul is only a temporary and constantly changing combination of sensations, emotions, and the like, and will cease to exist at death, just as a chariot no longer exists when you remove the wheels and axle and the other parts. Whatever we may think of this doctrine, its startling anticipation of modern psychology, which has often been remarked, shows clearly the Buddha's power of analytical thought.

But if there is no soul, what can transmigration mean? Here is one of the great puzzles of Buddhism. Those who know most about it seem least disposed to give a simple, definite explanation, so it behooves the rest of us to walk warily. Buddhist theologians have worked out elaborate expositions of the problem, but to attempt an outline of them here would only make confusion worse confounded. We can say at least that in some sense, which we cannot closely define, there is a sequence of lives bound together by the law of Karma, the deed and its consequences. It is not the same person who is reborn in another body, but each life is determined by the lives which preceded it in the series. Buddhists use the illustration of a candle which is lighted from another candle: the second flame is not the same as the first, but is caused by it.

Western interpreters have compared this Buddhist belief to the "immortality of influence." A still closer parallel would be our idea of heredity. Conceivably a Buddhist who accepts the point of view of modern science might re-interpret his belief in Karma as denoting the power of influence and heredity, by which every life profoundly affects many other lives. The great difference is that heredity and moral influence do not proceed in a direct and single line of succession. If every individual had just one child, and every child had only one parent, then heredity would be much more like the Buddhist conception of transmigration.

Yet neither heredity nor influence can correspond exactly to the Buddhist belief. The succession of lives does not follow the line of physical descent, but moves from one family, class, or nation to another, and direct influence is out of the question because the new life does not begin until after the one preceding it has ended. Furthermore, some kind or degree of identity is presupposed by the claim that a person who has attained enlightenment can remember all his former incarnations.

The conception of Nirvana is another puzzle in Buddhist belief. Literally the word Nirvana means extinction or blowing out, as a light is blown out, but what it is that is extinguished is not altogether clear. Is it personal existence or only sorrow? The Jainas claim that Buddhism teaches annihilation of the soul, which they deny, but the Buddhist

Nirvana is not the annihilation of the soul, because there is no soul. The enlightened saint, who is free from sorrow, is said to have attained Nirvana in this life. The term, therefore, does not necessarily mean the extinction of personal existence. Nevertheless Gautama's conception of the self seems to imply that death is the end of all conscious existence.

We cannot here go into the subject more deeply. If our presentation is not clear and consistent, neither is the doctrine itself. As a matter of fact, there is much disagreement about it among the Buddhist theologians, and Buddha himself left no answer to the question—it is the sort of question which he was content to leave unanswered, while he devoted himself to things of more immediate concern. Whatever else Nirvana may or may not mean, it is the end of sorrow, and that was all Gautama wanted.

We have already seen that his personal religious experience and his thinking were rooted in an overwhelming sense of the misery of life. When the great solution came to him under the Bo-tree, it took the form of what he called the Four Noble Truths, and the first of these was the fact of suffering. Any religion worthy of the name must take cognizance of this fact. The other side of the picture need not be forgotten, but to ignore the existence and the universality of pain and sorrow is both superficial and selfish. A story which recalls Thomas Hood's poem, *The Song of the Shirt,* is told in the Buddhist scriptures. A woman whose only son had died went about asking for medicine to cure him. The people thought she was mad, but one man sent her to the Buddha, who told her to bring him a handful of mustard-seed from a house where grief had never come. The poor woman went about from house to house, but every family had known bereavement. One night, as she sat by the roadside watching the lights of a city, it came to her that she had been selfish in regarding her grief as different from what others suffered. She therefore had her dead child buried and went and took refuge in the Buddha.

Since the first point in Buddha's teaching is the prevalence of sorrow, and his primary purpose is the eradication of sorrow, the second of the Four Noble Truths has to do with the cause of sorrow. This Gautama found in desire or craving. We sometimes say that if a man does not expect anything he will not be disappointed. Back of this rather flippant saying is the truth which Buddha had in mind. If we did not want anything, we should not grieve at not having it or at losing it. If our hearts were not set upon the things which life so often denies us, being deprived of them would not produce sorrow. In other words, the real cause of our trouble is not what happens to us but the way we take it. Poverty, disease, old age, and death, with all the other ills that flesh is heir to, are not in themselves necessarily productive of unhappiness; they become so because we *care,* because we *desire* wealth and health and youth and life.

From this follows the third great truth: the way to eradicate sorrow is to eradicate the desire which causes it. The resemblance between this idea and the Stoic doctrine of "apathy" is striking. For the Stoics too the chief end of life was to rise above fate and circumstance, and the way to do this was to cultivate insensibility to pain and sorrow. Nothing that life can do to us, said the Stoic, can hurt us unless we let it. The slave Epictetus, tortured in the rack by a cruel master, says, "If you twist that leg any more it will break"; and when it does break, he smiles and says, "I told you so." Now Buddhism does not seem quite so desperately heroic as Stoicism, yet the fundamental idea is the same. Get rid of desire and you abolish sorrow.

Of course the aim and the result are purely negative. The possibility of a positive joy to be achieved at the cost of pain, and worth the cost, does not even come into mind. The Buddhist ideal is not (theoretically, at least) that of one "who for the joy that was set before him endured the cross." Joy is not to be desired; escape from sorrow is the most that can be expected. Neither is the ideal one calculated to encourage the improvement of social conditions. Why strive to abolish poverty or disease? Seek rather the inner peace which is independent of the body's welfare. To be sure, Buddhism is not the only religion which has ever sounded this note. As a matter of fact, in practice Buddhism has often produced both positive joy and active social interest. It teaches absolute unselfishness, and this unselfishness has inevitably found expression in joyful service. As has so often and so fortunately been the case in Christianity, the religion of the Buddhists has been better than their theology. Someone has said that they have followed the example instead of the teaching of their founder. Nevertheless the theory remains fundamentally pessimistic. Christianity, when it has despaired of this world, has hoped for happiness in the world to come; Buddhism offers no hope of happiness either here or hereafter. Some would say that herein it has been the more rational and the more unselfish of the two religions, but however that may be, its teaching is that sorrow is man's lot until he learns to escape it by the extinction of desire.

The most distinctive point in Gautama's teaching is his conception of the way to do this. The last of the Four Noble Truths is that the way to uproot desire is neither worldliness nor asceticism, neither self-indulgence nor self-mortification, but a Middle Way, described in detail as the Eightfold Path. This doctrine sprang immediately out of Buddha's experience, as great religious ideas always do. Neither princely wealth and pleasures nor the most austere self-denial had brought him peace; the way he found lay between these two extremes. Judged by our ideas, to be sure, it seems decidedly ascetic, as we shall see when we consider the steps of the Eightfold Path and the vows of the Buddhist order. It is still true in Buddhism, as in Jainism, that salvation is only for the monk; one cannot walk the path of deliverance until he has renounced the ties of family and society. After all, Gautama was a child of India. Nevertheless, as compared with the accepted ideals of ancient India, the sanity and common sense and the audacious independence of his teaching are astonishing. Over against the teaching of Mahavira, for example, Buddha's Eightfold Path is indeed a Middle Way.

As the first of the Three Jewels of Jainism is faith in Mahavira as the Conqueror, so the first step in the Eightfold Path of Buddhism is Right Belief, the belief that Buddha's analysis of the cause of suffering is true, and his way of escape is the true way. Believing this, the seeker after salvation must exert his will and resolve to put his faith into practice, therefore the second step is Right Resolution. The outcome of this resolution must be Right Speech and Right Conduct, the third and fourth steps respectively. What is involved in Right Conduct we shall see presently.

Right Occupation, the choice of a vocation which demands no cruelty or sin, is required as the fifth step, and the sixth is Right Effort, or moral self-discipline and self-improvement. So far the path may be called a programme of ethical culture; the two remaining steps pass over into the realm of inner spiritual development and experience. Right Meditation, the seventh step, is the systematic training of the mind in the conquest of desire and sorrow, while the eighth step, Right Absorption, is the rapture of the mystic trance, Nirvana on earth.

The ideal of conduct is made explicit by ten vows, of which five are taken by laymen as well as monks and the remaining five by the monks alone. Destruction of life, theft, unchastity, falsehood, and the use of intoxicants are renounced by both monks and laymen. In some respects these sins are less strictly defined for the laity than for the monks: the vow of chastity, for example, involves celibacy for the monk but not for the layman, just as in Jainism. The first four vows are the same as the first four vows of the Jain monk. In the place of the Buddhist prohibition of intoxicants, the fifth vow of Jainism renounces personal attachments. In addition to the five general vows, the Buddhist monk also binds himself to abstain from eating after noon, participation in worldly amusements, the use of perfumes and ornaments, sleeping on raised beds, and accepting money.

Surely the strictest Puritan or Methodist could hardly accuse Buddha of worldly laxity, if these vows correctly represent his teaching. Whether they do or not we cannot be sure, for there were disagreements in the order even before the death of Gautama, some of his followers considering him too strict and others holding that he was not strict enough. No middle way is satisfactory to everybody, as the many controversies and schisms of Buddhist history eloquently testify. The general character of the ideal, however, is reasonably clear. It was a rather mild type of monasticism, as monastic ideals go, but still monasticism.

That the practical fruits of Buddhism have not been altogether negative from the point of view of social welfare has already been shown. The most distinctive emphasis in Buddhist ethical teaching is the emphasis on gentleness and mercy. Non-resistance and pacificism are characteristic of the Buddhist peoples of Asia, though not in extreme forms. It is said that the Buddha was once asked whether wrongdoers should be punished, and whether war was ever justifiable. He replied that punishment was necessary, but it should be administered without ill-will or hatred, and that war was sometimes unavoidable, but the aggressor was to be blamed.

European and American converts to Buddhism, of whom there are not a few, claim that Buddhism is the ideal religion for a scientific age, because it makes no demands upon faith. The first of the Four Noble Truths, they say, is a fact of observation: the existence of suffering is undeniable. The second and third truths follow from this logically, and the fourth—the way of deliverance—can be verified by experience. Apparently Karma and transmigration are regarded as too obvious to need demonstration. The fact is that Buddhism, even in its simplest form, requires faith as much as any other religion does. The faith in Buddha expected of his followers is not contrary to reason or superior to it, to be sure. He is trusted as the true teacher because he has the knowledge of experience; he can show the way to peace because he has been there, so to speak. At the same time Right Belief and Right Resolution are distinctly acts of faith, and no belief can be verified by experience until a man has faith enough to put it to the test.

It is quite true, however, that Buddhism appeals to the intellect. It calls especially for the exercise of analytic reasoning: as one writer has said it bids men see life steadily and whole by first picking it to pieces. The exercises prescribed for Right Meditation, for example, involve a detailed analysis of the objects of desire, emphasizing the most discouraging and distressing facts of life and death, with the avowed purpose of creating disgust and so abolishing desire—that is to say, killing all interest in life.

In the course of the centuries since the death of Gautama, Buddhism has spread through the lands to the east and north of India until it is now the greatest religion of Asia. In India itself it has practically died out, except in Nepal. We cannot here go into the developments and modifications which have taken place through all these centuries. They have been as many and as great as the corresponding developments and modifications of Christianity. Just as the personality of the historical Jesus has often been almost forgotten, and he has become in the minds of his followers hardly more than a colorless theological abstraction, Buddhism also, in some of its branches, has exalted—or reduced—its founder to the position of a vague metaphysical entity having little or no relation to the great creative personality of Gautama. All of the founders whose lives we have studied thus far have been deified by their followers, but the process has not involved such elaborate theological constructions in the other religions as it has in both Buddhism and Christianity. In other ways too Buddhism has changed, especially in China, Tibet, and Japan, where it has become an organized religion with gods, temples, priests, and ceremonies, all of which were lacking in the order as established by Gautama. But Gautama has not been forgotten. His influence persists, and not Asia only but all mankind owes him more than can be measured or expressed.

CHAPTER SIX

ZOROASTER

AGGRESSIVE MONOTHEIST

AGAIN we take in hand the pilgrim's staff and make our journey to another land, this time a land to the northwest of India, comprising what is now Persia and some of the adjoining countries. In ancient times this land was inhabited by a people of the same stock as those whose ancestors had migrated into India from this same region, and who had become the ruling race in India. In religion as well as in race the ancestors of the Persians were closely related to the Aryan conquerors of India. The gods to whom the hymns of the Rig-Veda are addressed were worshipped by the Persians also. The same myths were told by both peoples. Sacred fire played an important part in the religions of both, and the priests who attended it bore the same name with only a slight dialectic change. In both religions, also, a sacred drink was used in worship and again the names used for it show a common derivation: Soma in India, Haoma in Persia.

In India, as we have seen, the depressing climate, among other causes, produced a pessimistic, world-weary type of religion. Now on the high Iranian plateau the climate was more invigorating and more severe; life there was a constant struggle, and the religion reflected the difference in the life of the people. Not peace in a state of deliverance from the fear of rebirth, but prosperity in this world was the goal of endeavor, as it had been at first for the invading

Aryans in India. The good life was not a life of separation from all normal social relationships, but active participation in the struggle with nature and human enemies. The saint was not the ascetic, but the man who was a good farmer and cattle raiser, a good husband and father, a good warrior and citizen. The philosophy of life that inspired these Persians was positive and aggressive. All existence, the course of nature and the history of the universe as well as the life of mankind, seemed to them to be a struggle between a kingdom of good and a kingdom of evil, a kingdom of light and a kingdom of darkness, a kingdom of truth and a kingdom of falsehood. The warfare was not one of impersonal, physical forces; two opposing hosts of spirits, the angels and the demons, were engaged in cosmic strife. Man's participation in the conflict, therefore, required not only moral conduct and strenuous activity, but also the observance of many rites designed to avoid or to get rid of demonic pollution. The moral side of religion, however, was strongly emphasized.

Such was the spiritual environment into which Zarathustra—or, as we more commonly call him, Zoroaster—was born. Tradition gives the date of his birth as 660 B.C., something over half a century before the birth of Lao-tze in China and Mahavira in India, and exactly one hundred years before the birth of Buddha, who was born just a few years before Confucius. Many scholars, however, maintain that the actual date of Zoroaster's birth was considerably earlier than the tradition indicates, perhaps as early as 1000 B.C. or even earlier.

His followers believe that before his birth Zoroaster existed in heaven as the equal of the archangels. His advent on earth was foreseen in a vision and foretold three thousand years in advance. Again, three hundred years before it occurred, it was predicted by an ox, which for that purpose had been given the power of speech. Before the prophet's birth his Guardian Spirit and his Bodily Nature were marvellously combined with "the awful kingly Glory, made by Mazda," which belongs to the archangels "and to the blessed ones, born or not yet born, who are to perform the restoration of the world"; which also through many generations had united with great rulers and priests but had been vainly sought by wicked men; which "belongs to the Aryan nations, born and unborn," and which in the end "will cleave unto the victorious Saoshyant," the coming Savior. This divine Glory descended upon Zoroaster's mother, Dukdaub, at her birth, and produced such wondrous manifestations of its presence during her girlhood that the neighbors accused her of witchcraft, and her father had to send her away to another village. The man to whose care he entrusted her had a son named Porushaspo, who in due time became the husband of Dukdaub.

One day, after their marriage, the young husband went out to the riverside to wash their clothes. There he saw, growing out of the top of a tree, a marvellous stem of Haoma, the plant from which the sacred drink was made. Now in this Haoma stem the archangels had placed the Guardian Spirit of Zoroaster. They had then given the stem to two birds, and when some serpents attacked the birds' young, "that Guardian Spirit of Zoroaster smote them on the jaws, and the serpents fell down and expired." The Haoma stem was miraculously connected with the top of the tree, and "there, where the nest of the birds was, it grew constantly fresh and golden-colored." So Porushaspo found it, and, when he had finished washing the clothes, he secured it and took it home to his wife.

The Bodily Nature of Zoroaster was conveyed to his parents by another marvel. The archangels mixed it with "cloud-water," which fell gently upon the pasture where Porushaspo kept his cows, and two heifers, after eating of the plants upon which it had fallen, began to give milk and were milked by Dukdaub. Finally Porushaspo pounded the wondrous Haoma stem and mixed it with the milk from the heifers, and he and Dukdaub "drank up that Haoma and milk." The conception of their child followed. All through this strange process the demons strove again and again to interfere, but in vain. Thus the divine glory was joined to Zoroaster's body and spirit, and throughout his life it "clave unto the holy Zarathustra, so that he thought according to the Law, spake according to the Law, and did according to the Law; so that he was the holiest in holiness in all the living world, the best ruling in exercising rule, the brightest in brightness, the most glorious in glory, the most victorious in victory."

Before the child was born his mother was frightened by a dream that she was being attacked by wild beasts, but an astrologer whom she consulted predicted that her child would have a great career. Other marvels took place, and when the child was born he laughed, instead of crying, and pronounced a formula which put the demons to confusion. Evil sorcerers and the officers of a wicked ruler attempted to destroy him, though one of them admitted that it could not be done. His father was beguiled into assisting in an attempt to burn him to death; efforts were made to have him trampled by oxen and horses; he was exposed in a den of wolves. Through these and other perils the babe passed safely, but the hostility of demons and sorcerers pursued him through childhood. One day when he was seven years old, as he was building a hut with some other children, two of the evil magicians again tried to bewitch him, but although the other children were terrified, Zoroaster remained calm and unharmed.

It is not surprising to read that Zoroaster was a precocious child. With remarkable sagacity he disputed, sometimes rather violently, with his foes, the sorcerers, and stared them down when they attempted to destroy him with the evil eye. During his early childhood, up to the age of seven, he was instructed by a learned man in the Avesta, the sacred book of Zoroastrianism. (The fact that the Avesta was not yet written must not be allowed to spoil the story, and, besides, some parts of it may actually be older than Zoroaster.) Later, as a young man, he showed an eagerness to learn even from the wicked, but used discretion in what he accepted. Being once in an assembly of men who were noted for their wisdom, he asked them what was most favorable to the soul and was told that it was "to nourish the poor, to give fodder to cattle, to bring firewood to the fire, to pour Haoma juice into water, and to worship many demons." The first four he gladly did, but he refused to worship the demons.

At the age of fifteen Zoroaster joined his four brothers in asking their father to divide the family property among them, but for his own share he chose only a girdle. Since the sacred girdle is one of the symbols of Zoroastrianism, it is thought that his choice was intended to signify his devotion to religion, or even that it represents a formal rite of confirmation. Be that as it may, his thoughts were evidently not all of religion. He desired a good wife and was not easily pleased, for when his father found a girl for him, he "argued with the bride" and said, "Show me thy face, so that I may find out . . . whether its appearance be undesirable." The maiden—whether through bashfulness or anger is not stated—turned away, whereat Zoroaster said, "Whoever takes away a sight from me does not practise respect for me." Unfortunately the story does not tell whether he married this girl or not, though we know that he was no believer in celibacy; in fact, as we shall see later, he had three wives in all.

The beginning of his activity as a prophet of religion seems to have been preceded by a period of seclusion and quiet reflection. A Greek writer asserts that Zoroaster kept silence for seven years; Pliny tells us that he lived on cheese for twenty years in desert places. According to some of the Christian church fathers, he lived in a cave on a mountain. The Zoroastrian scriptures say that at the age of twenty he left home and wandered about the country inquiring for the most righteous of men, and, on being directed to a certain man, went to him and helped him minister to the poor.

Several examples of Zoroaster's active kindness are related. Once he found on the bank of a stream seven women and old people who were unable to cross; he therefore helped them over "in the manner of a bridge"—just how is not clear. Once, during a famine so severe that the livestock "constantly ate off the tails of each other," he distributed some of his father's supply of fodder among the neighbors' animals. What his father said is not on record. Again, seeing one day a starving dog with five puppies, he hurried to bring it food, but the animal died before he could reach it.

The decisive spiritual experience which determined the subsequent course of Zoroaster's life came to him when he was thirty years old. One day, it is said, when he was carrying Haoma water, he was met by the archangel Vohu Mano (Good Mind), who asked him what was his supreme desire. Zoroaster replied that it was righteousness. Another expression of his chief aspiration, which may be connected with the same experience, occurs in the Gathas, the portion of the Avesta attributed to Zoroaster himself. They relate that in response to a question from the messenger of God Zoroaster said, "To the wicked would that I could be in very truth a strong tormentor and avenger, but to the righteous may I be a mighty help and joy, since to preparations for Thy Kingdom, and in desire for its approach, I would devote myself so as to Thee, O Mazda, I may give praise and weave my song." Vohu Mano, on receiving Zoroaster's reply, brought him into the presence of Ahura Mazda (Wise Lord), the divine ruler of the kingdom of light, truth, and righteousness. Observe the suggestion of the story: Good Thought leads to God. Undoubtedly the actual experience which this story reflects was one of spiritual enlightenment after profound reflection.

This vision of Ahura Mazda, like Isaiah's vision of Jehovah in the temple, constituted Zoroaster's call to be a prophet. When he returned from it he began to preach to the priests of the old religion, who listened to him until he began to advocate the marriage of near relatives, at which

they demanded his death. The local ruler, though uncon-
verted, protected him. So, at least, says the legend. His-
torically it is more likely that the Persian custom of mar-
rying near relatives was not taught by Zoroaster himself
but was introduced in later times. In the course of the next
several years Zoroaster had an individual conference with
each of the six archangels in turn. Including the first meeting with Ahura Mazda, there were seven conferences in
all in the space of ten years. In these seven visions Zoroaster received the answers to seven important questions of
faith. It is said that he had these experiences in the various
places where he spent the winter months during these ten
years. Doubtless the stories reflect successive achievements
of insight after prolonged and deep reflection in the winter seasons.

But like Buddha after his enlightenment under the Bo-
tree, and like Jesus after his baptism in the Jordan, Zoroaster had to meet also a great temptation. The powers of
darkness strove to turn him from his path, but, again like
Jesus, he put them to flight with quotations from the sacred
scriptures of his people. Several instances of demonic as-
saults are reported. One time a female fiend came to him in
the form of one of the archangels. From the front her appearance was very deceiving, but Zoroaster made her turn
her back, thus exposing her real ugliness and the loathsome
reptiles crawling over her. There is keen psychological insight in these old stories, for temptations are always less deceiving if we turn them around and look at both front and
back.

During all these years Zoroaster had gained not a single
follower, and it was not until ten years after his first great

spiritual experience that his own cousin became his first convert. Discouraged by such a small beginning, he turned again to Ahura Mazda for renewed vision; then for two more years he strove again to win men to the truth as he saw it. Finally, at the age of forty-two, he came to the court of a certain King Vishtaspa. Here, in a three days' debate, he vanquished the king's wise men. The priests of the court, to discredit him, had things which were used by sorcerers placed in Zoroaster's room and then discovered there, and he was imprisoned on a charge of sorcery. It chanced, however, that one of the king's horses fell sick. The royal household was so stricken with grief that Zoroaster's jailer forgot to take food to him until the evening. Hearing then what was amiss, Zoroaster offered to cure the horse on condition that the king and queen and their son would accept his religion and investigate the wicked conduct of the priests. The story goes on to tell in detail how the horse was cured, one leg at a time, and the priests were sent to execution. The reader who knows his Bible can hardly fail to be impressed by the parallels between this story and those of Joseph and Daniel in the Old Testament. The conversion of Vishtaspa was the turning point in the history of the religion. Zoroaster sealed it by a solemn ceremony, which was followed by the most miraculous consequences for the king and his family. Though many of these details are clearly legendary, the conversion of Vishtaspa is undoubtedly an historical event.

Following the example of the king and queen, the royal court now adopted Zoroaster's teaching, which soon began to spread throughout the land. The king's counsellor married Zoroaster's daughter, and the vizier gave his daughter to Zoroaster in marriage. Zoroaster now had three wives. By them he had three sons and three daughters. Five classes of wives were recognized by the law; Zoroaster's second and third sons were the children of a "serving wife," while the mother of the first son and the three daughters was a "privileged wife." The third wife, the daughter of Vishtaspa's vizier, had no children, but by a strange miracle she is to be the mother of three sons of Zoroaster who will be born in the future, as the end of the world draws near.

Other conversions followed the winning of Vishtaspa and his court, and the religion began to spread. The king himself was zealous in extending the faith and fought two wars in its behalf. Stories are told of the conversion even of Hindus and of a Brahman sage who came to Vishtaspa's court to refute the doctrines of Zoroaster. Greeks also are said to have been converted. Zoroaster was kept busy preaching, organizing, acting as the chief priest of the new religion, and founding fire-temples, until his death at the age of seventy-seven. He is said to have been killed, while serving at the altar, by the eldest of five brothers belonging to the class of wizards or false priests who had been Zoroaster's deadly enemies ever since his childhood. If we accept the traditional date of his birth, his death occurred in 583 B.C., three years after Nebuchadnezzar captured Jerusalem and carried the Jews captive to Babylon. Curiously enough, one of the Zoroastrian books actually refers to Nebuchadnezzar's expedition against Jerusalem in connection with an obscure reference to a book which is believed to have been the Talmud. Also, granting the accuracy of these dates, Zoroaster's public activity occupied almost exactly the same years as that of the prophet Jeremiah; indeed there is a Jewish legend to the effect that he was a pupil of Jeremiah.

In character and personality Zoroaster was a man of a different type from any of the founders whose acquaintance we have made. With all the sincerity, earnestness, and perseverance that we find in any of them, and with a kindness toward the poor and toward animals recalling the compassion of Buddha, he combined a passionate aggressiveness which sometimes led him into unrestrained bitterness toward his enemies. Like many of the greatest saints of all religions, he seems to have been subject to alternate moods of enthusiasm and discouragement. His teaching reveals both profound moral insight and remarkable intellectual power, especially when we remember in what an early period of human history he lived.

Zoroaster did not, like Lao-tze, write a book, nor are his teachings preserved for us in the form of sayings like those of Confucius or sermons like those attributed to Buddha, but we have what are believed to be his own words in one of the oldest portions of the Avesta, a collection of seventeen psalms or hymns known as the Gathas. In them we find expressed the prophet's ardent devotion to Ahura Mazda, the revelations which he received from Ahura Mazda, the fundamental conclusions to which his deep reflection led him, and his lofty ethical ideals. While the form and purpose of the Gathas preclude a systematic presentation of Zoroaster's teaching, they are our chief means of distinguishing between his own conceptions and those which were developed or adopted by the religion in later times.

In the most ancient accounts Zoroaster seems to be regarded as a reformer of the old religion rather than the founder of a new one. He was not, however, like Confucius, merely a transmitter and preserver of old forms. Once more we are forced to recognize that every new religion grows out of an older one, either as a further development or as a revolt. Zoroaster inherited and accepted the aggressive, positive world-view of the ancient Persians and the conception of religion as participation in the cosmic struggle. Reverence for the sacred fire and the use of the sacred drink also are found in later Zoroastrianism and were probably accepted by Zoroaster, though the sacred fire is only incidentally referred to in the Gathas and the Haoma is not mentioned at all.

Zoroaster's originality appears chiefly in his rejection of the natural polytheism of the older religion. He was, first and last, a prophet of monotheism. The older gods he regarded as demons. From this change in attitude arose a curious fact in the history of language, the fact that our words *deity* and *devil* have ultimately the same derivation. In the ancient scriptures of India the gods were called *devas,* meaning "shining ones." The Latin *deus* comes from the same root, and from this we get the word *deity.* The Persians also used the same word for the gods, and when Zoroaster condemned these gods as demons they were still called by the same name; hence our word *devil.*

Zoroaster did not invent a new god to take the place of the older deities but exalted as the Supreme Being a god already worshipped among the others. Ahura Mazda was probably at first a sky-god, perhaps originally identical with one of the sky-gods of the old Indian pantheon. But Zoro-

aster not only set the Wise Lord above all other divine
beings; he also made paramount the ethical character of
Ahura Mazda as demanding righteousness of his worshippers. In the cosmic struggle of the two contending
realms of good and evil man's part is above all to live a
righteous life, though belief in the true God and ritual
purity are also necessary. In his almost exclusive emphasis
upon the moral aspect of religion, as well as in his jealous
loyalty to the one God, Zoroaster has often been compared
with the Hebrew prophets.

Closely connected with Ahura Mazda are the so-called
archangels, whom we have met frequently in the story of
Zoroaster's life. They are Vohu Mano (Good Thought),
Asha (Right), Kshathra (Sovereignty), Armaiti (Devotion), Haurvatat (Welfare), and Ameretat (Immortality).
While these Amesha Spentas (Bountiful Immortals) appear in the stories as personal beings, their names show
plainly that they are not old nature-deities but personified
ideas, and this fact rather strongly suggests that they were
Zoroaster's own invention, though of that we cannot be at
all sure. At any rate they are strictly subordinated to
Ahura Mazda, for he alone is God. They represent his attributes, the qualities which he requires of his worshippers,
and the blessings which he confers upon them.

Over against the kingdom of good is the kingdom of
evil, with its demonic hosts under the command of the evil
spirit, Angra Mainyu. In the later development of Zoroastrianism Angra Mainyu came to be regarded as of almost
equal power with Ahura Mazda, and the strife of good
and evil was regarded as by no means one-sided, though the
ultimate victory of the right was never doubted. With Zoro-

aster himself, however, this moral dualism was not so pronounced; the origin of evil and its relation to the power and goodness of God are not worked out in the Gathas, but there is no suggestion that the evil spirit even approaches the position of God's rival for the control of the universe.

The difference between these beliefs and those of any of the religions of China or India is sufficiently striking without further comment. Equally distinctive is the conception of the hereafter which we find in Zoroastrianism. The reader will notice also that in these and in other respects the religion of Zoroaster is much more closely related to Judaism and Christianity than are the religions of the countries farther to the east. Taoism and Confucianism are not concerned with the fate of the soul after death; Karma and transmigration, with Moksha and Nirvana, we leave behind us when we depart from India. But the most fundamental difference between the Zoroastrian view of the other life and the beliefs of these other religions is inherent in the basic conception of the universal conflict of good and evil, calling for man's most strenuous endeavor, but certain to result eventually in the victory of truth and righteousness. Jainism and Buddhism have no hope for the redemption of the world. Life is at best a necessary evil, and the only hope of deliverance from evil is for the individual who attains deliverance from life itself. Zoroastrianism offers no such counsel of despair; it challenges man to take his part in the battles of the invincible Lord of lords, looking to a universal redemption in the end. Needless to say, this does not mean that righteousness will gradually prevail over evil in human society on the earth as we now know it. Zoroastrianism, like early Christianity, looks not for an ideal social order in this world but for "a new heaven and a new earth, wherein dwelleth righteousness." Its hope is that of the apostle Paul: "Creation itself also shall be delivered from the bondage of corruption into the glorious liberty of the children of God."

Zoroastrian theology depicts the past and future history of the world in the form of a cycle of twelve thousand years, comprising four successive ages of three thousand years each. The last of these ages began when the prophet received his first great revelation. It is divided into three divisions of a thousand years each: the first of these is known as the millennium of Zoroaster; the second and third are named after two of the sons to be miraculously born to Zoroaster; and at the end of the third millennium will appear his third expected son, the Savior, Shaoshyant. The destined course of the millennium of Zoroaster is said to have been revealed to the prophet in a vision under the symbol of a great tree. The seven branches of the tree, which were made of seven diverse metals, represented seven periods in the history of the religion, or seven great persons who would appear in these successive periods. In what seems to be an earlier form of the story there are only four branches, "one golden, one of silver, one of steel, and one mixed." This representation of historical periods by different metals recalls Nebuchadnezzar's dream of the image with a golden head, silver breast and arms, brass belly and thighs, iron legs, and feet of mingled iron and clay, all of which Daniel interpreted as referring to the powerful empires which succeeded one another in the control of Western Asia. The books in which the Zoroastrian story has been preserved

are of later date than the Book of Daniel, but we cannot
be sure that the Zoroastrians borrowed the story from the
Jews. Certainly the details of the doctrine cannot be attributed to Zoroaster himself; it may be, however, that the
basic idea of a world-year, with twelve world-months of a
thousand years each, was actually a part of the prophet's
own teaching.

At the coming of Shaoshyant the dead will be raised.
The belief in a general resurrection at the end of the world
is one of the most characteristic doctrines of Zoroastrianism.
One cannot but remark the strangeness of the fact that two
religions originally so closely related as those of ancient
India and Persia should have developed beliefs so radically
different as those of transmigration and resurrection. Here
again the difference may be connected with the variant
points of view regarding the worth of life. The expecta-
tion of a reunion of soul and body is in keeping with the
emphasis upon the value of the present life in Zoroastrianism, while the idea of a relationship between soul and
body so loose that the soul may wear out and cast off one
fleshly garment after another accords well with the Indian
attitude of contempt for the flesh and its desires.

It is said that Zoroaster inquired of Ahura Mazda how
the body could be raised again after its dissolution. The reply was that to restore a body which had once existed would
not be so difficult as had been its creation out of nothing in
the first place. But the matter is not left in such obscurity.
We are told that the various constituents of the body are in
the keeping of various parts of Nature. The bones have
been delivered to the earth, the blood to the water, the hair
to the plants, and the life to the fire, and all will be re-

stored at the last day. The resurrection will be followed by
the judgment. The dead will be brought together and the
righteous separated from the wicked, and after a brief
period of reward and punishment a stream of molten
metal, which the righteous will feel only as warm milk,
will purify the earth and even hell itself. The Evil One
and all his hosts will be vanquished forever; all things will
become new.

As the scheme of world history has been elaborated by
later theologians, so has Zoroaster's teaching regarding the
destiny of the individual soul. In its developed form the
doctrine includes not only the resurrection and final judgment, but also a preliminary judgment at death and an
intermediate state of joy or suffering. The faults and
virtues of the soul are weighed, somewhat as in the ancient
Egyptian religion, and then the soul must meet the ordeal
of crossing a bridge, which narrows to the thickness of a
razor-blade when the wicked try to cross, but widens out
for the righteous. The delights of the pious and the torments of the unrighteous are depicted vividly in later
Zoroastrian literature. There is even a state of equilibrium
for those whose faults and merits are equally balanced. In
the teaching of Zoroaster himself, so far as we can judge
from the Gathas, the judgment of the individual and the
final destruction of the powers of evil were not separated.
The state of the soul between death and the day of judgment does not seem to have exercised the mind of Zoroaster, who was absorbed in the thought of the final consummation. In other words, the same development took
place in Zoroastrianism which we find in Christianity, beginning within the New Testament itself. Jesus had noth-

ing to say of the interval between death and the establishment of God's kingdom, but Paul found it necessary, since the Lord had not yet come again, to give comforting assurance to those whose loved ones had fallen asleep. One important difference between Christian and Zoroastrian doctrine must be noted, however. For orthodox Christianity heaven and hell are places of eternal reward and punishment, but for Zoroastrianism they are only the temporary abodes of the servants of Ahura Mazda and Angra Mainyu respectively. Hell, in other words, is only Purgatory, and the Zoroastrians are Universalists.

The condition of salvation was for Zoroaster, as we have already seen, righteous conduct. Here again the later followers of the prophet have somewhat modified his teaching, for they have added a mass of ceremonial requirements which sometimes almost overshadow the original demand for righteousness. Scholars are inclined to attribute this incursion of ritualism to the Magi, a tribe who became the priests of the religion not many centuries after Zoroaster's death. In spite of the increased emphasis on forms and rites, however, the ethical standards of Zoroastrianism have remained very high and have retained their characteristic stress on the positive social virtues. Typical of the Zoroastrian point of view is the opposition to asceticism expressed in the statement, "No one who does not eat has strength to do the works of holiness."

The virtue most emphasized is purity, involving freedom from both moral and ceremonial defilement. Honesty also is highly stressed: Zoroaster spoke of hell as "the world of the Lie." As might be expected from the fundamental point of view of the religion, kindness and charity are major virtues. One of the Zoroastrian books contains a striking parallel to a familiar gospel saying: "Whoever gives anything to the disciples of Zoroaster, his reward and recompense are just as though the thing had been given by him to Zoroaster." It is said that the Parsees, as the Zoroastrians in India are called, give more to charity *per capita* than any other religious group in the world.

Like Jainism, Zoroastrianism has not now very many adherents. Indeed in numbers it is the least of the world's great religions, only about one-tenth as large as Jainism. Hardly ten thousand Zoroastrians remain in Persia; many were driven into India by Mohammedan persecution, and their descendants, the Parsees (*i.e.,* Persians), now number about one hundred thousand. Like Jainism, also, the religion has ceased to be an aggressive missionary faith claiming to be the true religion for all mankind, and has become hereditary and exclusive. Yet none of these facts affect the greatness of Zoroaster himself or his position in the spiritual history of mankind. His conception of the one true God of righteousness, and of man's struggle against evil as one phase of a gigantic conflict in which all the universe is involved, must be regarded as of the highest importance, both intrinsically and by virtue of the influence these ideas have had on other religions. Judaism, and Christianity and Mohammedanism as the daughters of Judaism, cannot afford to be ungrateful to the prophet of Ahura Mazda.

CHAPTER SEVEN

MOSES

EMANCIPATOR AND LAWGIVER

THE difficulty of deciding whether or not a certain individual should be considered the founder of a religion is well illustrated by the case of Moses. The Bible says that Abraham, Isaac, and Jacob had worshipped Jehovah before Moses' day; indeed it says of the time of Seth, the son of Adam, "Then began men to call upon Jehovah." Judaism and Christianity have commonly regarded Abraham rather than Moses as "the father of all them that believe," for he is said to have left his father's home in Haran, where they worshipped other gods, and to have journeyed to Canaan at the command of Jehovah. Then again, if we look for the most important advances in the development of the Hebrew religion, we see that many of them took place after the time of Moses. Even the belief that there is only one God was not reached until many centuries after his lifetime. Moses taught the *worship* of one God only, but the gods of the other nations were long supposed to be as real as the God of Israel.

The reason for calling Moses the founder of the Hebrew religion is that he definitely made Jehovah the national God of the Hebrew people as a whole and established the beginnings of a religious as well as a political organization. Some of the tribes which later formed a part of the Hebrew nation had worshipped Jehovah from time immemorial;

others had not known him—or, as the Bible puts it, had worshipped him under other names. It may be said that Moses was a reformer rather than a founder, but the same thing may be said of so many of the other founders that we need not stop here to draw a line which, as we noted at the beginning of our study, can be only an arbitrary one at best.

The time of Moses' birth cannot be exactly determined. We cannot even be sure in what century he lived, though the range of possibility is hardly as wide as in the case of Zoroaster. One thing may be said with some degree of confidence, that, unless the traditional dates of Zoroaster's life are more than half a millennium too late, Moses was the earliest of all the founders of our present-day religions. He certainly lived well before the year 1000 B.C.; some recent writers think 1500 would be nearer the mark. The date most commonly accepted by Old Testament scholars is about 1200 B.C.

Whatever may have been the date, the Hebrews at the time of Moses' birth were suffering oppression and slavery in Egypt. Since the coming of their ancestors in search of food, they had multiplied until the ruling Pharaoh had become afraid of them and had ordered that no more male children among them should be allowed to live. Under such conditions of distress and danger Moses was born. Jewish legend says that his birth came three months ahead of the normal time, that his mother suffered no pain, and that he was born circumcized. In defiance of the royal decree, his mother hid him for three months; then, finding such concealment no longer possible, she placed him in a watertight basket made of bulrushes and cast the tiny bark adrift on the waters of the Nile. His sister Miriam kept watch to see what would become of him. When no less a person than the daughter of the king, coming down to the river to bathe, discovered the baby there, Miriam boldly stepped forward and offered to find a nurse to take care of the child for the princess. The nurse she found was of course the baby's own mother. It is interesting to note that a story in some respects much like this is told in an ancient clay tablet about Sargon, who ruled in Babylonia more than a thousand years before the time of Moses. In later centuries the Greeks also had many stories of boys who were exposed and rescued, and who became great men.

When Moses was three years old, according to Jewish legend, his mother brought him to Pharaoh's daughter, who accepted him as her own son. On being brought into the presence of Pharaoh the child lifted the crown from the monarch's head and placed it on his own. The wise men of the court declared that a prince so anxious to reign should be strangled, but on the advice of Job, whom the legend conveniently finds at Pharaoh's court at this time, Pharaoh decided that if the little Moses had acted without realizing what he was doing, he should be allowed to live. A crude intelligence test was therefore devised: the child was offered a plate containing gold and another filled with burning coals, to see how wisely he would choose between them. He at once stretched out his hand toward the gold, but to avert disaster the angel Gabriel moved the little hand to the plate of burning coals, one of which Moses seized and carried to his mouth. That, say the rabbis, is why Moses was heavy of speech all his life.

The most thorough education was given the adopted prince. The New Testament says that he was "learned in all the wisdom of the Egyptians and was mighty in words and in deeds." The Jewish philosopher Philo, who lived in the time of Jesus, maintained that Plato and the other great thinkers of Greece had derived what was true in their teachings from Moses. The rabbis have a beautiful story to the effect that Moses was taught at Pharaoh's court the names of all the gods of Egypt, but at night remembered his mother's songs about a God who was invisible and omnipresent; he learned the glorious history of Egypt, but at night his thoughts were of the enslaved Hebrews; he learned the duties of princes and kings, but at night he remembered his mother's saying, "Be prudent like Jacob, be gentle like Isaac, be faithful like Abraham."

When he was old enough to take a prince's part in warlike exploits, he was given charge of a campaign against a city which many generals had tried in vain to capture. It was protected on two sides by strong walls and on another side by a river, while a field full of serpents prevented access from the fourth side. Moses ordered his soldiers to capture a great number of ibises; these with their beaks both blinded and killed the serpents, and so the city was conquered.

Neither education nor military success obscured the young man's consciousness of his origin. At length his loyalty to his own people was put to the test. "And it came to pass in those days, when Moses was grown, that he went out unto his brethren, and looked on their burdens; and he spied an Egyptian smiting a Hebrew, one of his brethren. And he looked this way and that way, and when he saw that there was no man, he slew the Egyptian and hid him in the sand." Somehow the deed became known, as Moses discovered the following day when he presumed to intervene in a quarrel between two Hebrews. The man whom he held to be in the wrong replied angrily to his rebuke, "Who made thee a prince and a judge over us? Intendest thou to kill me, as thou killedst the Egyptian?"

Soon the matter came to Pharaoh's ears, and Moses fled into the desert. But, like Jacob when he fled from the face of Esau, in the desert he found romance. One day he came to a well in the land of the Midianites, where the seven daughters of Jethro, the priest of Midian, came to draw water for their father's flocks. Just as Jacob had rolled the stone from a well's mouth and had watered Laban's flocks for Rachel, so now Moses helped Jethro's daughters when the rough shepherds of the region rudely drove them from the well. As a reward for his chivalry he was invited to make his home with the priest. One of the seven daughters, Zipporah by name, became his wife and bore him a son, whom he named Gershom (A Stranger There).

So for some time Moses lived in the land of Midian, keeping the sheep of his father-in-law. By keeping sheep, the rabbis say, he learned how to shepherd God's people. Legend dwells lovingly on this period of his life, giving instances of his loving care for the sheep which remind us of the New Testament picture of the Good Shepherd. One day as he was leading the flock through the desert, Moses came to a mountain known as "the mountain of God." Here a wondrous sight met his eyes: "the Angel of the Lord appeared unto him in a flame of fire out of the midst of a bush; and he looked, and, behold, the bush burned with fire, and the bush was not consumed." When Moses drew near to see the marvel more closely, a divine voice from the burning bush warned him to put off his sandals and come no nearer, for the ground on which he stood was holy. Then God spoke to him of the affliction of the Hebrews in Egypt and charged him to return boldly to Pharaoh and demand in the name of Jehovah that the Hebrews be released.

Just what happened that day on the mountainside we cannot know, any more than we can know exactly what happened at similar crises in the lives of other great saints and prophets. Perhaps Moses had a vision; or perhaps the burning bush is but the symbol of a new flame of insight and consecration in his own heart. Certainly one of the great religious experiences of history occurred then, whatever form it took or however we may choose to account for it. Then and there Moses came to know God for himself and received the consciousness of his life's great mission. He hesitated, we are told, and no wonder. Only a small man can take a big task lightly. The answer to his hesitation was the assurance that God himself would be with him. He was told that on this same mountain he and the people of Israel would worship their divine Deliverer. One objection after another which he raised was answered. Finally he urged his lack of eloquence and was told that his brother Aaron would be his spokesman.

One reason for Moses' hesitating to accept his task was the fact that he had not known God before in this way. He did not even know the name of the mighty Deity who appeared to him, for he said, "Behold, when I come unto the children of Israel and shall say unto them, The

God of your fathers hath sent me unto you, and they shall say to me, What is his name? what shall I say unto them?" In reply God said, as our English Bible renders it, "I am that I am," or as we should put it in modern English, "I am what I am." He continued, "Thus shalt thou say unto the children of Israel, I AM hath sent me unto you." The connection between this and the name Jehovah is not apparent in English, but it is essential to the meaning of the passage.

As a matter of fact, the form *Jehovah,* in the English Bible, does not accurately represent the Hebrew name. What its original form really was we do not know with certainty, but probably instead of *Jehovah* we should write *Jahveh,* or better still *Yahweh.* In this form the name resembles very closely the Hebrew for "He is." If such was its meaning, Moses was sent to the Hebrews by the God HE-IS, the Eternally Existing One. Still more likely is it that in the original Hebrew text the word had a causative form and significance, meaning "He Causes To Be." We might then translate God's reply to Moses in this way: "I Cause To Be That Which Is, and you shall say to the children of Israel, HE CAUSES TO BE (*i. e.,* the Creator) has sent me to you."

In saying that this is apparently what the name meant to Moses we do not imply that it was the original meaning. The name Yahweh, though previously unknown to Moses, was by no means new even at that early date. Babylonian records show that a deity of this name had been worshipped for many centuries before Moses' time by some of the Semitic peoples of western Asia. This agrees with the biblical statement that men began to call upon Jehovah in the days of Seth. Yet we read that the name was unknown to Abraham, Isaac, and Jacob. The most probable explanation of these facts is that the Midianites whom Moses' father-in-law served as priest were worshippers of Yahweh as the God of the mountain on which Moses was pasturing the flock when his vision came to him. To be sure, there are verses in the biblical account which read as though Jethro accepted the religion of Jehovah only after Moses had led the Israelites out of Egypt, and Judaism has regarded him as its first proselyte. Nevertheless the mountain where Moses saw the burning bush is called the mountain of God, and probably had that name before God appeared to Moses there; moreover the account of the relations between Jethro and the Israelites indicates, on the whole, that it was he who taught them how to worship Yahweh, as would naturally be the case if he was a priest of the God who had made himself known to Moses.

If a hypothetical reconstruction of Moses' experience may be allowed, we may imagine something like this. In Egypt he had seen a religion which, though based upon idolatry and polytheism, had developed a very high type of thought regarding the chief of its gods, the Sun. One of the hymns of this religion contains these lines:

"Hail to thee! O disk of day,
     Creator of all and giver of their substance."

A Pharaoh of the fourteenth century B.C. even attempted to establish a thorough-going monotheism, worshipping the sun as the sole Lord and Creator of the universe. Possibly Moses was acquainted with this short-lived but noble-minded reform. A stanza of one of its hymns reads as follows in the translation of Professor Breasted:

> "O sole God, whose powers no other possesseth,
> Thou didst create the earth according to thy heart
> While thou wast alone:
> Men, all cattle large and small,
> All that are upon the earth."

It is natural to suppose that Moses would reflect upon such lofty conceptions as these and upon their relation to the religion of his own people. Then during his sojourn with the priest of Midian, whom he respected and whose daughter he married, he would become acquainted with the God of the mountain on which his sheep found pasture, the God whose name was Yahweh. No great effort of imagination is needed to picture him, in the solitude and quiet of the shepherd's life, pondering upon the three religious conceptions thus given him by his experience: the faiths of the Hebrews, the Egyptians, and the Midianites. Somehow he must have come to the conviction that the God of his wife's people was one and the same as the God of his own forefathers, though the latter had not known him by the same name.

Then, we can imagine, the similarity between the name Yahweh and the Hebrew (or Aramaic) verb meaning "he causes to be" would come to him with the force of a discovery, and he would say to himself, "Not the Egyptian Sun-god but Yahweh—*He* it is that has created all things; *He* brings into existence; *He* causes to be!" Combined with his troubled thoughts about the plight of his people in Egypt and the stirrings within him of a conviction that he should go back and lead them to freedom, the new sense of the greatness and power of God which these other reflections brought him would constitute a profoundly moving experience. If such was indeed the course of his thoughts, no wonder he felt the glow and elation of a great spiritual discovery. No wonder Nature itself seemed aflame on the mountain of God. No wonder he brought his people straight to this same mountain from Egypt and established there an eternal covenant between Yahweh and Israel.

Whether or not this is what really happened, Moses at once secured the consent of Jethro and set out with his wife and his two sons to return to Egypt. On the way occurred an incident which serves to remind us from what a hoary antiquity and from what a primitive stage of religious development the whole story of Moses has come down to us. "And it came to pass by the way in the inn, that Yahweh met him and sought to kill him." The danger was averted by the prompt action of Zipporah, who seized a sharp stone and circumcized their son, Gershom, saying to Moses, "Surely a bloody husband art thou to me!" What is the meaning of this strange story, which reflects such a crude and savage conception of God? Was circumcision a rite of Jethro's people unknown to the Hebrews before they adopted the worship of Yahweh? Had Moses neglected this rite, and is that why it is said that Yahweh sought to kill him? We cannot tell. Perhaps a severe illness befell Moses on the way back to Egypt, and Zipporah put this interpretation upon it. Circumcision is said to have been established by a covenant between God and Abraham, but we are also told that the Hebrews in Egypt were not circumcized.

Meanwhile Aaron, Moses' brother, had been moved to come into the desert seeking him. They met at the mountain of God and went back to Egypt together. Presumably Zipporah returned with the children to her father's home, for we hear no more of her until Moses brings the escaped Israelites to Yahweh's mountain, when she comes to meet him with her father and her two sons. Arrived in Egypt, Moses and Aaron gathered together the elders of Israel and told them of the divine purpose to deliver them from the oppressive power of Pharaoh. The promise was confirmed by signs which God had given Moses in connection with the revelation from the burning bush. Moses' rod, when cast upon the ground, became a serpent, but when he took it up again it was a rod as before. His hand, when he placed it in the bosom of his robe, became white as with leprosy, but when he placed it again in his bosom it was restored to its normal condition. Seeing these signs and hearing the Lord's command as Aaron eloquently presented it, the people trustingly accepted the promise of deliverance and "bowed their heads and worshipped."

It was not so easy to persuade Pharaoh to let them go. Time and again Moses and Aaron appeared before him and in the name of Yahweh demanded that the Hebrews be allowed to go three days' journey into the wilderness and there sacrifice to the Lord, but, in spite of the wonders which they performed to substantiate the divine origin of their commission, the cruel monarch was deaf to their appeal. The plagues which fell upon Egypt as punishment for this hardness of heart need not here be related in detail. Many of them can be explained by natural phenomena, but the story naturally grew with repetition through many gen-

erations. It would seem that Moses appeared in a time
when Egypt was suffering the calamities that often accompany a change in government. The early part of the six-
teenth century B.C., when the Hyksos or Shepherd Kings
were driven out and the empire was established, was such
a time; so also was the latter part of the thirteenth century,
when the empire was breaking up under the repeated attacks of invaders from the north. Invasion, followed by
pestilence and famine, would provide an opportunity which
the Hebrews might well accept as providential.

When Pharaoh's own son perished in the fearful pestilence that smote the Egyptians, he acceded to the demand
of Moses and Aaron. That very night the children of Israel
made their escape. Staff in hand, loins girded, their shoes
on their feet, they ate a hasty meal while the pestilence
raged in the homes of Egypt. No Hebrew house was
touched by the deadly plague, for in accordance with
Moses' instructions the Hebrews had marked the lintels
and side posts of their doors with the blood of the lambs
which they killed for their last meal in Egypt, and the
destroyer passed over every house so marked. Therefore
the yearly commemoration of that memorable night is
called the Passover. So the children of Israel began their
journey; "and a mixed multitude went up also with them,
and flocks and herds, even very much cattle." Of their
borrowing jewels and raiment from the Egyptians before
their flight, and so spoiling the Egyptians, the less said
the better.

The straight road from Egypt to Palestine led along the
shore of the Mediterranean Sea, but that was the route taken
by the armies of the Pharaohs when they invaded Asia, and

it was the route taken by the hosts of raiders from the north who from time to time invaded Egypt itself. Hence, when the people of Israel departed from Egypt, "God led them not through the way of the land of the Philistines, although that was near; for God said, Lest peradventure the people repent when they see war, and they return to Egypt: but God led the people about, through the way of the wilderness of the Red Sea." Another reason for journeying toward the east was that Moses wished to take the people to the mountain of God and introduce them to the worship of Yahweh. The Bible says that the Israelites were led by a pillar of cloud by day and a pillar of fire by night, and an eminent scholar has suggested that the mountain of God was a volcano far off on the eastern horizon, to which they were guided by the smoke it emitted in the daytime and by its red glow at night.

But much was to happen before they reached the holy mountain. Pharaoh had no sooner allowed them to escape than he regretted his decision and despatched an army after them. The children of Israel had just reached the shores of the Red Sea when they were overtaken by the pursuing chariots. The story of their marvellous passage through the sea and of the overwhelming of Pharaoh's hosts by the returning waters is too familiar to require repetition. Suffice it to say that the event was not necessarily miraculous, though certainly providential. The statement that "the Lord caused the sea to go back by a strong east wind all that night" involves nothing that would have to be considered supernatural in one of the long, shallow arms at the northern end of the Red Sea, which probably extended then into what is now a region of marshes and small lakes.

Naturally the escape was celebrated in song and story with such poetic expressions as we find in the obviously figurative statement, "And with the blast of thy nostrils the waters were gathered together, the floods stood upright as a heap." In this way we can account for the later idea that when the Israelites went through the sea "the waters were a wall unto them on their right hand and on their left."

After this great deliverance the people journeyed eastward again. The crucial importance of water to travellers through the desert is recalled by the story that after going for three days the Israelites could find no water except some which was too bitter to drink, but which Moses made sweet by casting into it a tree as the Lord directed him. The hardships of the journey and the longing of the people for the fleshpots of Egypt not only provide the setting for the familiar incidents of the coming of the quails and the finding of the manna, but also throw into high relief the perseverance and courage of Moses.

By taking the desert route Moses did not avoid entirely the necessity of fighting his way. The Amalekites, a nomadic people inhabiting the territory to the south of Palestine, disputed the passage of the Israelites through what they regarded as their domain. At this point in the story we meet for the first time a man who was destined to play a large part in the further progress of Israel through the wilderness and in the conquest of Canaan. Joshua, the son of Nun, appears at once as the military leader of the Israelites on this first occasion of warlike activity. The victory of Israel over the Amalekites, however, is not ascribed chiefly to the valor or leadership of Joshua. During the battle Moses stood on a nearby hill with the rod of God in his hand, and beside him stood his brother Aaron and one of the elders named Hur. "And it came to pass, when Moses held up his hand, that Israel prevailed; and when he let down his hand, Amalek prevailed. But Moses' hands were heavy; and they took a stone and put it under him, and he sat thereon; and Aaron and Hur stayed up his hands, the one on the one side, and the other on the other side; and his hands were steady until the going down of the sun." Thus the runaway slaves won a battle; they were now on the way to become a nation.

Soon after this they reached the mountain of God called sometimes Horeb and elsewhere Sinai. Here they were met by Jethro with Moses' wife and sons. At the mountain on which Moses had received his first revelation Jethro led in the observance of a sacrificial feast, introducing Israel to the formal worship of Yahweh. On the following day Moses sat from morning till evening judging the cases of those who brought their disputes to him for arbitration. Jethro, seeing that the mass of this work was too great for one man, offered a bit of wise advice which led to the first step in the definite organization of the people. Moses continued to be God's representative, declaring the divine will and judging the most difficult cases, but for all minor disputes subordinate officials were appointed. Having made these two significant contributions to the establishment of Hebrew law and religion, Jethro returned to his home.

What now follows is as momentous as the escape from Egypt. Yahweh and Israel were bound together by a solemn covenant, and in the name of Yahweh Moses presented to the people the Law, the very heart of the Hebrew religion from that day to this. The terms in which the mani-

festation of Yahweh is described irresistibly suggest a volcanic eruption: "Mount Sinai was altogether on a smoke,
because Yahweh descended upon it in fire; and the smoke
thereof ascended as the smoke of a furnace, and the whole
mount quaked greatly." The people stood at the base of the
mountain and were strictly forbidden to touch it, for the
ancient Hebrews held the primitive conception of holiness
as an awful force which destroys those who touch anything containing it. Moses alone went up into the immediate presence of God and received the Law. Then he built
an altar at the base of the mountain and offered sacrifice
upon it, after which he read to the people "the book of the
covenant" in which he had written the laws revealed to
him, and the people said, "All that the Lord hath said will
we do, and be obedient." The solemn compact was sealed
by sprinkling half of the blood of the sacrifice upon the
altar, representing God as one party to the agreement, and
the other half upon the people as the other party. So Israel
became the people of Yahweh, and he became their God.

Several times Moses went up into the mount. One time
he took with him seventy of the elders of the people, together with Aaron and his two sons, Nadab and Abihu.
"And they saw the God of Israel; and there was under his
feet as it were a paved work of a sapphire stone, and as it
were the heaven itself in its clearness." Doubtless this reflects a very simple conception of going up into the sky and
seeing God, yet it is noteworthy that the ancient Hebrew
historian refrains from any attempt to describe the appearance of God himself. Either at this time or on another day
—the connection in the narrative is not quite clear—Moses
took Joshua alone and went up into the mountain, leaving

Aaron and Hur in charge of the people. For forty days and forty nights Moses remained with God, and Joshua must have been somewhere near during all that time, for he was with Moses when the latter returned to the people.

The revelation of the Law was of such vital importance to Judaism that we need not be surprised to find the story of Moses' sojourn in the mount elaborated most marvellously by the rabbis of later times. Where the Bible says that Moses "went into the midst of the cloud," the rabbis aver that the cloud carried him into the heavens, and that after passing through all the heavens and seeing both the joys of the righteous and the torments of the wicked, as well as the angels and archangels and the Messiah who was to come at the end of days, he came to the school of the Most High, where he spent the whole forty days and forty nights studying the Law which he was to deliver to the people. But, being only a man, he forgot as fast as he learned; wherefore the Almighty took two tables of stone and on them wrote the Law for Moses. These tables, the rabbis say, could be read from the front or from the back. They were made of hardest sapphire, yet weighed nothing and could be rolled up like a scroll of parchment; moreover, though they were only six feet square, they contained not only the Ten Commandments but all the six hundred and thirteen commandments of the finished Law.

According to orthodox Jewish tradition, indeed, the Law revealed to Moses comprised, in addition to the written Law of Scripture, the unwritten Law, which for many centuries was to be transmitted only by word of mouth until it was finally written down in the Talmud. Modern historical scholarship sees in the laws of the Old Testament a complicated system bearing all the marks of long and gradual development in response to ever changing needs. Many of the precepts presuppose a settled agricultural or commercial life, and many have clearly been patterned upon the Babylonian laws which were known in Canaan before the Israelites settled there. Moses undoubtedly established the original nucleus about which these more developed forms of legislation clustered. The laws he promulgated would naturally be such as were needed for the nomadic life of the tribes during their wandering through the wilderness. But orthodox tradition recognizes no such gradual addition and expansion; it regards the whole Law, written and unwritten as well, as one and eternal. God himself, the rabbis say, obeyed the Law and consulted it when he created the world.

At the end of the forty days and forty nights God told Moses to return to the people, for they had departed from the true religion in his absence. Not knowing what had become of Moses, they had demanded that Aaron make new gods to lead them, and complying weakly he had made a calf of gold which they were now worshipping with shameful abandon. So great was Yahweh's indignation at this early defection from the solemn covenant that he threatened to destroy the fickle people and make a new nation of the descendants of Moses. But the prophet, before descending from the mountain, earnestly interceded for the people and so averted the wrath of the offended Deity. Then, bearing the two tables of the Law, he went down and with Joshua approached the camp. "And when Joshua heard the noise of the people as they shouted, he said unto Moses, There is a noise of war in the camp. And he said, It is

not the voice of them that shout for mastery, neither is it
the voice of them that cry for being overcome; but the
noise of them that sing do I hear. And it came to pass, as
soon as he came nigh unto the camp, that he saw the calf
and the dancing; and Moses' anger waxed hot, and he cast
the tables out of his hands and brake them beneath the
mount. And he took the calf which they had made and
burnt it in the fire and ground it to powder and strewed
it upon the water and made the children of Israel drink of
it."

Such fierce indignation ill accords with the prevalent
conception of Moses as the meekest of men. As in the instance of his slaying the Egyptian, he showed himself
capable of hot anger and violence, like one who in a later
age made a scourge of cords and drove the moneychangers
from the temple. The forcefulness of Moses' character is
strongly contrasted with the weakness of Aaron, who in
answer to his brother's rebuke said, "Let not the anger of
my lord wax hot: thou knowest the people, that they are
set on mischief." Ridiculous, like all weak excuses, is his
account of the making of the golden calf: "I said to them,
Whosoever hath any gold, let them break it off. So they
gave it me; then I cast it into the fire, and"—we can imagine the shrug of his shoulders and his deprecating smile
as he said it—"and out came this calf!"

The punishment of the people did not stop with their
drinking the water into which Moses had thrown the dust
of their idol. Standing in the gate of the camp Moses cried,
"Who is on the Lord's side? Let him come unto me." His
own tribe, the tribe of Levi, responded to the challenge and
ranged themselves by his side; then at his command they

drew their swords and strode through the camp wreaking fearful destruction on the unfaithful people. After this blood offering Moses went up again to the presence of God to plead for mercy. "Oh, this people have sinned a great sin," he said, "and have made them gods of gold. Yet now, if thou wilt forgive their sin—; and if not, blot me, I pray thee, out of thy book which thou hast written." His plea was granted, but "the Lord plagued the people, because they made the calf, which Aaron made."

Moses had destroyed the tables of stone on which God had written the Law, but he had not destroyed the Law. The rabbis say that when he cast the tables on the ground, the letters which had been divinely engraved upon them left the stone and flew back like birds to heaven, and the tables, bereft of the sacred writing, became heavy like any ordinary stone and were shattered on the earth. So now Yahweh commanded Moses to prepare two new tables and bring them up to the top of the holy mountain. There the glory of the Lord was revealed to the worshipping prophet. Moses had besought Yahweh to vouchsafe a more manifest vision of his glory, and Yahweh had replied that no man might see his face and live, but that he would allow his prophet to see his back. A crude conception of God is here displayed, yet the story is impressive in its majestic simplicity. As Moses stood in a cleft of the rock, Yahweh descended in a cloud and passed by, covering the prophet with his hand as he passed and then removing it so that his back might be seen. And as he went by Yahweh proclaimed his mighty name: "Yahweh, Yahweh, a God merciful and gracious, longsuffering and abundant in goodness and truth, keeping mercy for thousands, forgiving iniquity and transgression and sin, but that will by no means clear the guilty." Then God again confirmed his covenant with Israel and declared his Law, and at his command Moses wrote the words of the Law upon the tablets which he had brought with him. But these were tablets of earthly granite, and the writing was human writing, though the words were divine.

The time had now come to prepare to leave Mt. Sinai. Doubtless before this Yahweh had been thought of as a local god, the god of this volcanic mountain and the region surrounding it; but he had made his power felt in distant Egypt, and now he was to go before his people and lead them in the conquest of the promised land. Moses' contribution to the Hebrew religion consisted not only in establishing the worship of Yahweh as the religion of the nation, and in giving that worship its characteristic form as a voluntary covenant between the nation and its God, but also in freeing the conception of Yahweh from its local connection and thus preparing the way for the later thought of him as Lord of all the earth. Unfortunately, after Yahweh had conquered the nations for Israel and shown himself Lord of the land of Canaan as well as of the desert, the Hebrews came to think that his power was as much confined to Palestine as ever it had been to the region surrounding Mt. Sinai. It was left for the prophets of much later days to declare boldly that all the nations were tools in Yahweh's hands.

As the symbol of God's constant presence wherever his people might go, Moses prepared the ark, a wooden chest containing the tables of the Law. A portable sanctuary, known as the tabernacle or tent of meeting, was also constructed, and in this Moses was wont to commune with God after Mt. Sinai had been left behind. "And the Lord spake unto Moses face to face, as a man speaketh unto his friend." When he came down from the mountain after the second giving of the Law, we are told, Moses' face shone so that the people were afraid to look at him; therefore, when he had finished declaring the Lord's commandments, he put a veil over his face. "But when Moses went in before Yahweh to speak with him, he took the veil off, until he came out. And he came out and spake unto the children of Israel that which he was commanded. And the children of Israel saw the face of Moses, that the skin of Moses' face shone; and Moses put the veil upon his face again, until he went in to speak with him."

Of the journey through the wilderness from Mt. Sinai not many incidents need here be repeated. The hardships of the journey caused much murmuring among the people. Even Moses' own sister Miriam, who had guarded his floating cradle when he was a helpless baby, and his brother Aaron, who had been his spokesman before Pharaoh and was now the first high priest of Israel, were jealous of his authority and pre-eminence. The immediate occasion of their defection is said to have been Moses' marriage with an Ethiopian woman: perhaps this was a second marriage, but there is no other mention of a second wife, and the Hebrew word translated "Ethiopian" has in reality a wider meaning and might include Zipporah, the Midianite. As in all cases of such obscurity and uncertainty in the Scriptures, the rabbis have many theories and stories to fill the gap in our knowledge. The underlying cause of the rebellion, in any case, was envy. The anger of Yahweh at this unworthy disloyalty was manifested by afflicting Miriam with leprosy. At Moses' intercession she was healed, but for seven days she had to be shut out of the camp.

It is in connection with the foregoing incident that Moses is described as "very meek, above all the men which were upon the face of the earth." The setting of the statement makes clear its meaning: not a lack of the capacity for righteous indignation is implied, but a sublime superiority to personal resentment. When he killed the Egyptian and when he so fiercely punished the worship of the golden calf, it was not a personal offense that aroused his wrath. He was meek in the sense that he had no petty concern for his own position. An incident which occurred just before the rebellion of Aaron and Miriam reveals his spirit. The gift of prophecy had been conferred upon the seventy elders of the people on a particular occasion; all but two of them were with Moses at the tabernacle, but these two began to prophesy among the people in the camp. When word was brought to Moses that what had been his peculiar prerogative was being exercised by two others in the camp, Joshua urged him to forbid them, but Moses said, "Enviest thou for my sake? Would God that all the Lord's people were prophets, and that the Lord would put his Spirit upon them!"

On the southern border of Canaan the tribes halted for some time at an oasis named Kadesh. From this place Moses sent twelve men to reconnoitre and report upon the nature of the country and the prospects for obtaining a foothold in it. All but two of them (Joshua and an elder named Caleb) brought such a discouraging account of the strength of the Canaanites that the people lost heart and dared not attempt an invasion. Their lack of courage was punished by a divine decree that for forty years they should have to continue their nomadic life in the desert. All that generation of escaped slaves, excepting only Joshua and Caleb, was doomed to die in the wilderness. The ultimate conquest of Canaan was made by a new generation, born in the desert, inured to desert life, disciplined in war and in the co-operation demanded by freedom, and nurtured from birth in the fear of the Lord.

During the sojourn at Kadesh Miriam died. Further complaints among the people and attempts at revolt against the authority of Moses tried his patience sorely. A shortage of water was met by bringing water out of a rock, but somehow in connection with this incident—just how the narrative does not make clear—Moses and Aaron were guilty of a lack of faith in Yahweh which was punished by the decree that they, like the rest of their generation, should die without having entered the promised land.

Turning sadly away from the border of Canaan, the children of Israel now made their way eastward. To the southeast of Canaan lay the kingdom of Edom, and Moses sent word to the Edomite king requesting free passage through his territory. It was refused. Too weak or too fearful to attempt a passage by force of arms, Israel turned farther to the south and journeyed clear around the domain of the Edomites. On the way, at Mt. Hor, Aaron died, and his son Eleazar succeeded him as high priest. A plague of fiery serpents, sent as punishment for continued murmuring and revolt, was healed when Moses at the command of Yahweh held up before the people a brazen serpent, and those who had been bitten looked upon it. A strange survival of ancient serpent-worship, obscurely connected with the worship of Yahweh, seems to be reflected here. Many centuries later the brazen serpent was worshipped in the temple. It was destroyed by King Hezekiah.

Having passed the land of Edom and turned again to the north, the Israelites encountered further opposition, but now they were stronger and fought their way through the armies of the Amorites and Moabites to the plains of Moab. What happened there—how Balaam blessed the children of Israel instead of cursing them; and how the undoing of Israel, which neither force nor magic could accomplish, was almost brought about by the Moabite women—is it not written in the Book of Numbers?

When the Israelites camped on the banks of the Jordan, the borders of the promised land had been reached again, and the forty years of wandering were over. Moses could go no farther. Forewarned that his end was near, he solemnly consecrated Joshua as his successor, saying to him, "Be strong and of a good courage, for thou must go with this people unto the land which the Lord hath sworn unto their fathers to give them, and thou shalt cause them to inherit it. And the Lord, he it is that doth go before thee; he will be with thee, he will not fail thee, neither forsake thee: fear not, neither be dismayed." After thus consecrating his successor and having written out the Law and entrusted it to the Levites, Moses went up to the top of Mt. Pisgah, from which he could look over into the land which his feet might not tread upon. There he died, and "no man knoweth of his sepulchre unto this day."

Some of the stories told by the rabbis picture Moses in his last days as a feeble old man, cringing in terror before the thought of death. Very different is the word of Scripture: "And Moses was a hundred and twenty years old when he died: his eye was not dim, nor his natural force abated." Joshua carried on and completed the work of bringing Israel into Canaan, but Joshua was not Moses. "And there arose not a prophet since in Israel like unto Moses, whom the Lord knew face to face, in all the signs and the wonders which the Lord sent him to do in the land of Egypt, to Pharaoh and to all his servants and to all his land, and in all that mighty hand, and in all the great terror which Moses showed in the sight of all Israel."

What we know of the Hebrew religion as instituted by Moses may be told very briefly. Its central and dominating idea was that of the covenant between Israel, as the chosen people, and Yahweh, "a jealous God" who demanded the exclusive allegiance of his worshippers, and a holy God who required not only sacrifices and the observance of festivals but also a life of rectitude. The Law which Moses gave was not the elaborate legal code of the finished Pentateuch; the ritual and priesthood which he instituted did not include the details of the system worked out by the priests of the temple in Jerusalem; the social and moral laws which he established did not embody fully the ideals of the later prophets; and the conception of Yahweh which he taught did not involve the denial that other gods existed. Nevertheless the ideal of faithfulness to the covenant with Yahweh and the promulgation and administration of the Law in his name determined for all time the essential character of Judaism as the religion of the Law of God, and pointed the way to the full unfolding of ethical monotheism in the teaching of the prophets and of Jesus.

CHAPTER EIGHT

MOHAMMED

PROPHET OF THE ONE GOD AND OF JUDGMENT

ALL of the founders whom we have studied thus far lived in the sixth century B.C. or earlier. Between the latest of them and the lifetime of Mohammed there was a space of more than a thousand years, for Mohammed did not see the light of day until 570 A.D. Christianity was several centuries old, and had spread through most of western Asia and a considerable part of Europe. What is now called England was occupied by half a dozen little kingdoms of Saxons and Angles. The empire of Rome had fallen about a century earlier, but southeastern Europe and western Asia were still ruled by the Eastern or Byzantine Empire, which had its capital at Constantinople. Its chief rival was the strong empire of the Sasanians in Persia. The Persians were Zoroastrians; the Romans (as the people of the Byzantine Empire were still called) belonged to the Greek Orthodox branch of Christianity. In Arabia there were many Christians of this and the other eastern churches and also many Jews, but on the whole the people of that great and mysterious peninsula were polytheists and idolaters of a rather primitive sort; in fact they were not notably devoted to religion of any kind.

Mohammed's parents belonged to the tribe of Koreish, the most influential in the city of Mecca. One branch of this tribe had charge of the Kaaba, a little temple enshrining

a sacred stone to which pilgrims came annually from far
and near. So great was the popularity of Mecca as the goal
of countless pilgrims that it aroused the jealousy of the
Abyssinian Christians who then controlled Yemen, in
southern Arabia, and they attacked Mecca in the year of
Mohammed's birth. The fact that the invading army was
accompanied by an elephant, the first one ever seen by the
people of Mecca, made such an impression on them that
they afterwards spoke of that year as "the year of the elephant." The attack was a failure, however, because the
army, elephant also, was miraculously destroyed. A flock
of birds carrying stones in their claws flew over the soldiers'
heads, it is said, and dropped the stones on them; also a
remarkable downpour of rain swept the host away in a
raging torrent. According to a more modern and more
sophisticated theory, it was smallpox that destroyed the invaders.

Tradition relates that Mohammed's father was prepared
for the coming of his son by a drink from a marvellous
stream, which suddenly appeared before him one day when
he was in the region of Mt. Ararat, and which as suddenly
disappeared after he had drunk of its remarkably clear, cool
water. During the months preceding the child's birth his
mother was guarded by an angel; she was also informed of
the future greatness of her son and was told the name to
be given to him. The divine favor bestowed on her was
further shown by a supernatural brightness emanating from
her body and visible even at a great distance from Mecca.
Marvellous visions were given her, and wondrous portents
accompanied the birth of the child: idols fell, thrones were
turned about, kings were struck dumb for a day, sorcerers

lost their power. The boy's father, however, was not present to see these things. He had gone off on a trading expedition, and died away from home before his son was born.

Following the custom of the Arabs, the baby was not nursed by his mother but by a woman belonging to a Bedouin tribe, who took him to the tents of her own people and took care of him for five years. Thus he learned to speak the pure Arabic of the Bedouins. Two or three times during this period his nurse was alarmed by a strange affliction which seized the child. Some think this was epilepsy; certainly Mohammed was of an extremely nervous temperament and suffered some kind of nervous disorder, perhaps a kind of hysteria. When he was only six years old his mother died, and he was cared for by his grandfather, who was very fond of him. A few years later the grandfather also died; after that Mohammed grew up under the care of an uncle. It is said that his uncle took him to Syria with a trading caravan. If so, he probably saw something of Judaism and Christianity there. He would also naturally see something of both these religions during the fairs at Mecca. There is a tradition, indeed, to the effect that he heard a Christian bishop preach at one of these fairs. Judging by his attitude in later years, he seems to have been impressed by the quarrels between Jews and Christians, but he also observed that they had a Book which both revered as sacred, and that both Jews and Christians worshipped one God.

The family fortune had been spent in all too generous provision for the needs of pilgrims, and Mohammed's uncle was unable to support him entirely after he was able to work for himself. As a boy he was employed as a goatherd. In after years he said, "Verily there hath been no prophet raised up who performed not the work of a shepherd." In his youth he is said to have been unusually handsome but of exemplary virtue. Stories are told of his miraculous deliverance from the temptations incurred by his physical attractiveness.

When he was old enough to be entrusted with greater responsibility, his uncle secured for him a position as manager of a caravan belonging to a wealthy kinswoman, a widow named Khadija. His ability and success in this enterprise won the esteem of Khadija, and when she met him on his return a real and mutual affection sprang up which led to their marriage. Mohammed was at this time twenty-five years old, and Khadija was forty, yet the match was a good one not only financially. Khadija brought Mohammed a sympathetic understanding and a confidence which were of priceless help in the years that followed. He, on his part, loved her deeply and had no other wife during the quarter of a century that they lived together. Two or three sons —accounts differ as to the number—were born to them but died in infancy; their four daughters all lived to maturity and were married.

In physique Mohammed is said to have been of about medium size, lean but with broad chest and shoulders. His head, which was covered with thick, black, curly hair, was large; his brow was broad, and there were veins on his forehead which swelled when he was angry. His eyebrows were arched and joined together; his eyelashes were long and black; his black eyes were bloodshot and restless. A ruddy complexion, an acquiline nose, teeth that were large and of sparkling whiteness, and a black beard marked a face that has been characterized as sensuous but intelligent. He walked quickly and with a slight stoop as though climbing a hill. His temperament was inclined to melancholy, though he sometimes laughed so heartily that he had to hold his sides and his teeth and gums were visible. A man of strong passions, he usually kept himself under control. His kindness to his friends was as notable as his fierce, vindictive hatred of his foes.

Marriage brought with it sufficient worldly goods to afford more leisure than Mohammed had previously enjoyed. He was thus able to indulge his fondness for solitary meditation. During the first fifteen years of his married life he practised fasting and lonely vigils—probably in imitation of the Christian hermits and monks, since the Arabs were not given to such usages. An intense inner struggle was going on, for Mohammed was searching with passionate earnestness for the true religion. Doubtless what he had seen of Judaism and Christianity made him dissatisfied with the religion of his fellow countrymen. What he heard of a coming judgment particularly impressed him. There were also some Arabs who already believed in one God; two of these Inquirers, as they were called, were relatives of Khadija, and another was a neighbor.

When Mohammed was thirty-five years old there occurred an incident which may have suggested to him, as some believe, the thought that he was to be a religious leader. The Kaaba, the shrine containing the ancient sacred stone at Mecca, was injured by a flood and despoiled by thieves; in the course of its restoration a dispute arose between certain clans over the privilege of replacing the sacred stone.

An agreement was reached to accept as arbitrator the first man who should enter a nearby gate, and Mohammed was the man. He decided the dispute with the wisdom of a Solomon by laying the stone on a shawl and having a representative of each of the rival clans hold one corner of the shawl.

Five years later Mohammed received his first great revelation. He was meditating alone on a mountain near Mecca when the angel Gabriel appeared to him and said:

> "Recite in the name of thy Lord,
> Who created man of a clot of blood.
> Recite! Thy Lord is most gracious,
> Who taught man by means of the pen,
> Taught man what he knew not."

The statement regarding God's teaching man by the pen is clearly a reference to the Jewish and Christian scriptures. The verb here rendered "Recite" is the same as the Hebrew word meaning to call or cry, as in the verse, "The voice of him that crieth in the wilderness, Prepare ye the way of the Lord." The verb also means, in both Hebrew and Arabic, *to read*. There is a Jewish sect whose name, Karaites, is derived from it in this sense, because the adherents of this sect reject the Talmud and accept only what we call the Scriptures (literally, Writings), but what they call *Mikra* (that is, Readings). From this same root comes also the word Koran—hence this etymological digression. The Koran consists of the recitations or readings revealed to Mohammed; its original, the Mohammedans believe, exists eternally in heaven, and Mohammed only recited what was dictated to him.

In spite of the years of agonized groping for light which had preceded his vision, Mohammed was frightened by the light when it came. He did not know whether to accept it as a genuine revelation or to regard it as a sign of mental disorder. His hesitation does him credit. Khadija tried to calm and comfort him, but it was long before he overcame the haunting fear that he might be mad. For about three years no further revelations came. Mohammed was a prey to despair and seriously contemplated suicide. He was in the condition known to mystics as the Dark Night of the Soul, when vision fails and leaves the heart more desolate than it had been before it knew the bliss of illumination. Then one day the angel came again. In a panic Mohammed hurried to Khadija and, lying down, begged her to wrap him in his cloak. So he was accustomed to lie when afflicted by the strange attacks to which he had been subject since childhood. And now the angel spoke again:

"O thou enwrapped, arise and warn,
And magnify thy Lord!"

From then on the revelations came thick and fast. Khadija's confidence in their genuineness emboldened Mohammed to trust them, and he began to preach what had been given to him. At first he ventured to address only individuals of his own family and acquaintance. Others besides Khadija accepted him as a divinely ordained prophet. One of them was his cousin Ali, then a boy only ten years old; another was a prominent citizen named Abu Bekr. Both of these we shall hear of again. The influence of Abu Bekr was felt at once in the accession of further converts, and Mohammed began now to preach publicly. The burden of his message at this time was strict monotheism and the coming judgment. He denounced idolatry and other heathen practices, especially the custom of putting infant daughters to death.

For the most part this message was received with contempt, which was succeeded by active opposition when it became evident that the new doctrines would interfere with business. The annual influx of pilgrims was a source of considerable profit to the merchants of Mecca, who were therefore as devoted to the old deities as the goldsmiths of Ephesus had been to Diana in the days of Paul. Mohammed's uncle, who had brought him up from childhood, protected him, although not himself a convert to his nephew's teaching. Finding the family thus solidly behind him, his enemies undertook a boycott of the whole clan. The prophet himself was too well established to be seriously injured by such persecution, but some of his less wealthy followers suffered severely. A number of them he sent to seek refuge in Christian Abyssinia.

Then for a time he weakened. A revelation had come to him, he announced, permitting the worship of the three goddesses especially venerated in Mecca. At once the boycott was abandoned, and the refugees in Abyssinia gladly returned. But Mohammed had not yet reached the point where he could unblushingly receive revelations on the basis of mere expediency and self-interest. Stern conscience rebelled, and he decided that the compromising revelation had come from Satan; accordingly he bravely renounced it and declared again that there was only one God. The three goddesses, he said, were only names invented by the forefathers of the Meccans.

The persecution was now renewed, and to it was added personal sorrow. Khadija died in 619 at the age of sixty-four, leaving Mohammed, who was now forty-nine years old, without his first and most devoted supporter, well named by later generations the Mother of the Faithful. Only a year later his uncle too was taken from him. Mecca had become an unhappy place for the prophet, and he now began to turn his eyes elsewhere. With one of his disciples he visited another town, but he was rejected there and returned to Mecca. Meanwhile, however, he had made converts among the pilgrims as well as among the inhabitants of Mecca, and some of them had begun to spread his teachings in the city which is now known as Medina. Mohammed was invited by the authorities of this city to come and be their ruler. Naturally he accepted the invitation, but before leaving Mecca he saw to it that most of his followers there made good their escape and that they preceded him to the city which had proved more hospitable to his teaching. Just before his own departure a plot was made against his life, and he barely got away in time. For three days he hid in a cave with Abu Bekr, then slowly and cautiously the two made their way to Medina, which owes its name to the fact that from now on it was the City of the Prophet (Medinat an-Nabi). This flight is the great Hegira which marks the beginning of the Mohammedan era. It took place in 622 A.D., when the prophet was fifty-two years old.

In Medina Mohammed at once demonstrated on a larger scale the practical ability which he had shown as the manager of Khadija's caravan. He successfully united the tribes which constituted the population of the city and so became the ruler of a strong little state. With the Jews, of whom there were many in Medina, he was not so successful as with the Arab citizens. Believing as he did that his teaching was the true religion of Abraham, he hoped at first that the Jews would accept him as the successor of their own prophets. His revelations had been ascribing high honor to the Jewish religion, his followers were taught to pray with their faces toward Jerusalem, and he had appointed the Jewish Day of Atonement as a great annual fast day for all true believers. But the Jews would not accept him. They ridiculed his inaccurate versions of Bible stories. Mohammed retorted that he had received the stories by revelation, and the Jews had falsified their own Scriptures. Thereafter he instructed his disciples to pray toward Mecca instead of Jerusalem, and for the Day of Atonement he substituted the month of Ramadan. The change was important, for henceforward, in spite of much Jewish and Christian influence, the religion was a religion of and for the Arabs. The true religion of Abraham, Mohammed said, had not come down through Isaac to the Jews, but had been handed down among the Arabs through their ancestor Ishmael. More and more now Mohammed drew closer to the old Arab religion. He regarded the Kaaba in Mecca as the holy place of the true faith and determined to get control of it.

Meanwhile his flight to Medina had not ended the hostility between him and the people of Mecca. His followers had attacked caravans belonging to Meccan merchants and even pilgrims on their way to Mecca. Pitched battles took place, and Mohammed was victorious. At last, eight years after the Hegira, he gained possession of the city which had cast him out. The idols were destroyed, and the Kaaba became a Mohammedan shrine. As the power of the prophet grew, his ambition grew also. The policy of conversion by the sword was adopted. People of the Book, as Mohammed called the Jews and Christians, were spared, but idolaters and polytheists were put to death if they refused to be converted. In a few years Mohammed had become the ruler of the whole Arabian peninsula. He even sent messengers to the rulers of the Byzantine and Persian empires demanding submission and acceptance of the faith. Only his death, ten years after the flight from Mecca, prevented him from undertaking the conquest of these nations.

The character of Mohammed is one of puzzling contradictions, and therefore is peculiarly difficult to appraise justly. His profound religious genius is undeniable. He was the founder of what is to-day one of the greatest religions of the world, both in its extent and numbers and in the worth of its teachings. He was also a poet of no mean ability and—strange combination!—a remarkably able political leader. Unfortunately, as one who tries to judge him with an open mind is bound to confess, he was not quite big enough morally to be uncorrupted by success and power. Such power as his would spoil almost any man. In this respect the life of Mohammed recalls that of the ancient Hebrew king and poet, David. Both the character and the preaching of Mohammed degenerated more or less during the latter part of his life. The intense earnestness and the poetic fire of the earlier preaching gave way to a cooler and more prosaic style of utterance. What we cannot but consider a loss of complete sincerity appears in the fact that Mohammed's later revelations sometimes speak the dictates of self-interest and expediency rather than the oracles of profound spiritual vision. Even here, however, self-deception is more likely than conscious hypocrisy. If Mohammed was not always sincere in the fullest sense of the word, we have no right to say that he was an impostor. His failings were, at the worst, those of a man completely convinced that he was the chosen spokesman of God. We must remember also his restraint in never claiming a divine nature or miraculous powers.

In this connection we cannot ignore the rather unpleasant story of Mohammed's many marriages and complicated domestic relationships. For twenty-four years, as we have seen, he was true and devoted to Khadija, but after her death he fell captive to the charms of one woman after another—sometimes more than one at a time. The worst of it is that after prescribing for his followers the limitation to four wives he was able to receive special revelations allowing himself a larger number. Modern Mohammedan apologists are able to account for everything of this sort without admitting any loss or lack of nobility in the prophet, but their explanations do not quite ring true in our ears. At the same time in all fairness we must remember that the full facts of the case are not accessible to us, and there may be some justice in the claim of the apologists that all Mohammed's marriages, when not motivated by a natural desire to escape the reproach of having no son to survive him, are to be attributed to the praiseworthy motive of providing for widows and poor women whom he could not otherwise take under his personal care.

In any case we must give Mohammed credit for what he actually accomplished. There can be no question that he taught a much nobler religion than his people had known before, a nobler and truer religion, indeed, than some of the forms of Christianity then known and practised in western Asia. Social reforms as well as higher religious beliefs are attributable to him also. In particular—a fact which comes with surprise to most Occidentals—he improved and elevated the position of woman. The legal rights of women, especially with regard to property, are said to be higher under Mohammedan law than under the laws which prevail (or prevailed until recently) in some of our American states.

Mohammed wrote no book. Probably he was unable to read or write. The primitive religion of the Arabs in his time had no scriptures, and what he knew of the Jewish and Christian scriptures came only by hearsay. We have already noted that the contents of the Koran were revealed to him by angelic mediation and were delivered by him orally. During his lifetime these revelations were often written down by his followers on bits of palm-leaves or scraps of leather, but no systematic compilation was attempted until after his death. Who wanted a book while the living voice could still be heard, especially when fresh revelations sometimes contradicted and superseded those which had preceded them? The collection of the fragmentary records was made not long after the prophet's death, however, and it undoubtedly represents his teaching almost as well as if he had written the book with his own hand. No narrative of his life is added, neither are there hymns or prayers or any of the other elements frequently found in sacred books. The Koran consists entirely of the sayings of Mohammed.

The primary and all-controlling article of faith in Mohammedanism is the oneness of God. The noun Allah, by which Mohammed designated God, is not a proper name like Jehovah, but simply a form of the common Arabic word for a god. "There is no god but God, and Mohammed is his prophet"—that is the creed of Mohammedanism, the first of the "Five Pillars" of the religion. In character Allah is the God of the book of Job: omnipotent, omnipresent, and merciful, but the absolute and irresponsible Sovereign of the universe. The Christian doctrine of the Trinity seemed to Mohammed to be no better than polytheism, and undoubtedly for most of the Christians with whom he had any contact it amounted practically to a belief in three Gods, as it does with many uneducated Christians to-day. The idea that God could have a Son was to Mohammed outright blasphemy—of course he had no understanding of what the theologians meant by the doctrine. Jesus, according to Mohammed, was the last and greatest of the prophets before himself. God had in times past spoken to the fathers through the prophets and Jesus, and now through Mohammed, "the seal of the prophets." But he had not and could not speak through a Son, "the brightness of his glory and the express image of his person," for that would violate the essential unity of his nature and his transcendence over human life. "He alone is God," says the Koran; "God the Eternal. He begetteth not, and is not begotten; there is none like unto him."

Mohammed's consistent emphasis upon the unity and uniqueness of God prevented the deification of the prophet himself in orthodox Mohammedanism, though some forms of the religion have come rather near to it. The

Koran does not even claim for Mohammed the power of working miracles, but rather condemns, as Jesus did, the generation that asks for signs before believing. Of course it was not long before the true believers began to attribute miraculous powers to their prophet. Especially common were stories of his increasing supplies of food and producing water. On the whole, however, Mohammedanism has continued to regard its founder as a divinely inspired but purely human prophet.

The doctrine of the sovereignty of God was carried through by Mohammed into its corollary, predestination. In teaching this, however, he was not merely being logically consistent. His own experience led him to the belief that Allah hardened whom he would and had mercy on whom he would. Only so could he explain the fact that so many of the people who heard his message refused to accept it. In exactly the same way the apostle Paul arrived at his conception of the hardening of Israel: why was it that Israel would not accept its own Messiah, unless God had temporarily hardened their hearts in order that the Gentiles might receive the gospel? Orthodox Mohammedanism carries the doctrine of predestination further than Christianity has ever carried it, but in so doing it also goes beyond the teaching of its own founder. Second only to his emphasis on the unity of God was Mohammed's insistence upon man's responsibility for his own actions. The thought of a coming judgment was very real and terrible to him, and he said explicitly that God was not responsible for any man's sins, nor could a man evade responsibility by attributing his sinful nature to heredity. When the Westminster Confession of Faith asserts the

Calvinistic belief that God has eternally and immutably decreed whatsoever comes to pass, yet not so that man is bound to sin or free from responsibility for his sins, it only repeats the unresolved paradox which is implicit in the Koran as it is in the New Testament. Incidentally one may venture to remark that no philosophy has ever escaped this paradox except by ignoring some of the facts of human experience.

Judgment, we have said, was one of the cardinal points in Mohammed's teaching. Here, as elsewhere, Jewish and Christian influence may be discerned. The very word which Mohammed uses for the place of torment to which the wicked will be committed betrays a Jewish· background: Jehinnam is the Hebrew Ge-hinnom, or Gehenna. The fearful punishments to be visited upon the unrighteous are vividly pictured in the Koran, sometimes in terms that recall Christian teachings and sometimes in more original imagery. One passage may be quoted: "Verily, those who disbelieve in our signs, we will broil them with fire; whenever their skins are well done, then we will change them for other skins, that they may taste the torment. Verily, God is glorious and wise." Fetters, shirts of pitch, and boiling and filthy drinks are also mentioned.

The place of bliss to which the righteous will go has a Jewish name too, *viz.,* Paradise. The word is of Persian origin and was doubtless borrowed by Judaism from Zoroastrianism. In the description of Paradise Mohammed used more "local color" than he did in the pictures of Jehinnam. The dominant conception was that of "gardens beneath which rivers flow"—and what could be more enticing to the desert-dwelling Arab? Lying on soft couches and waited upon by lovely, large-eyed maidens, the righteous would enjoy abundant milk and honey, luscious fruits, sweet perfumes, and delicious wines. Christian writers have called this a sensuous if not a sensual picture, but in fairness it must be remembered that the wine leaves no headache and does not inebriate, and the lovely maidens "restrain their looks" and "come not nigh," though it is true that in one passage the Koran promises "pure wives" to the faithful in Paradise.

Scholars have remarked that the references to the large-eyed maidens occur in revelations which were given while Mohammed was living with the elderly Khadija, and that they drop out later when he had many wives. Whether this is to be explained by mere disillusionment in the later period or by a more psychoanalytical theory the reader must judge for himself. Professor W. H. Worrell has gone so far as to propose a Freudian explanation of Mohammed's whole religious experience. Pointing out that Khadija was fifty years old when Mohammed was only thirty-five, he says, "Mohammed developed poetry and prophecy in the later years of his marriage with Khadija, and lost both these gifts in the ensuing twelve or thirteen years when he made his many marriages." Mohammedan interpreters say that the later pictures of Paradise are more spiritual because Mohammed's own spiritual experience had grown deeper, and because it was no longer so necessary to use pictorial language as it had been when he first began to preach.

For Mohammed as for Zoroaster judgment presupposed resurrection. Descriptions of the day of resurrection and judgment in the Koran often recall the apocalyptic portions of the Old and New Testaments. Wonders in heaven and on earth will accompany the blowing of the trumpet; in every nation God will raise up a witness against it, just as Mohammed is a witness against the unbelievers among the Arabs; every man will be given a book with his deeds written in it; the wicked will be condemned and sent in troops to Jehinnam, and the righteous will be vindicated and sent in troops to Paradise. To doubters regarding the resurrection Allah gives the same answer that Ahura Mazda gave in answer to Zoroaster's question. "Does not man then remember," says the Koran, "that we created him before, when he was naught?" Both the miracle of human birth and the growth of vegetation on the earth are dwelt upon as evidences of the power of Allah which will bring about the resurrection.

The righteous, who will inherit Paradise, are those who believe the words of the prophet and do the will of Allah as he declares it. All this is included under the term Islam, which means literally *surrender,* or *submission.* As Taoism is named for its leading idea rather than its founder, so the religion which we commonly call Mohammedanism is named by its own adherents Islam. The believer in this religion is designated by the participle of the verb of which Islam is the infinitive: he is a Moslem, one who submits. The root meaning of this word is peace, and this is sometimes held to be the primary implication of the terms Islam and Moslem. A common English expression may help to make clear the connection between the ideas of peace and submission: we say that a man whose conscience is clear and whose faith is assured has "made his peace" with God. The fundamental idea is not so much helpless capitulation to the irresistible power of God as willing acceptance of the true faith and of the duties of a believer.

Mohammed's ethical ideals were high, considering the times in which he lived. Like the three other religions of ethical monotheism—Zoroastrianism, Judaism, and Christianity—Islam does not teach asceticism but a positive social righteousness. Almsgiving is one of the cardinal duties of the Mohammedan. The attitude of the Koran toward the use of alcoholic beverages differs from that of the New Testament, for in the former it is strictly prohibited. Slavery and polygamy are allowed, but the New Testament does not forbid slavery, and even in the matter of marriage Mohammed placed restrictions on the customary usage of his day and country. A religion of more refined ideals could hardly have succeeded among the Arabs, nor could it spread so rapidly among the primitive tribes of Africa as Mohammedanism is spreading to-day. Furthermore it would be unjust to forget the real advances made by Mohammed in many matters of moral and social practice. Unfortunately, as Professor G. F. Moore reminds us, by giving his teaching the finality of a divine revelation he made its imperfections as well as its virtues permanent, so that further social progress has been virtually impossible. In Moslem lands to-day any break with established social traditions is stubbornly resisted by the religious authorities.

The missionary zeal of its founder has not been lost by Islam as it has by Zoroastrianism and Jainism. With Christianity and Buddhism, Mohammedanism is one of the three great universal religions of the world to-day. It is growing faster at present than any other religion except Christianity. In the number of its adherents it is about half as large as

Christianity. The political character which Mohammed himself gave to the religion has never been entirely lost, although there is now no political unity among the Moslems and they have no official head. Until the World War the Sultan of Turkey was the Caliph of Islam, the successor of the prophet as the head of all believers, but since the war the caliphate has lapsed and in the new Turkish Republic religion has been disestablished. In spite of political reverses and social conservatism, however, the religion of Mohammed is decidedly alive. Like all living and growing religions it has experienced divisions and changes in the course of the centuries. In the Shia form, which is the state religion of Persia, it is as unlike the teaching of Mohammed as Japanese Buddhism is unlike the teaching of Buddha.

Even so the Koran preserves the founder's teaching in its original form. Mohammed is not only the latest of the founders of the great world religions but the best known as well. Legends a-plenty have grown up about him, but it is much easier to distinguish legend from history in his case than in the stories of the more ancient men whose lives we have hitherto examined. In the main events of his life and the main features of his character, as well as in his teaching, we can feel that we have sure and accurate knowledge of the fiery prophet of Arabia.

CHAPTER NINE

NANAK

SINGING EVANGELIST OF TWO COMBINED FAITHS

THE study of Nanak's life takes us back again to India. We find there, in some respects, much the same religious conditions which obtained in the days of Buddha and Mahavira, yet there are important changes also, for two thousand years have intervened between that time and the period in which Nanak lived. The caste system is more firmly entrenched than ever, and much more highly developed. The supremacy of the Brahman priesthood, the authority of the Vedic scriptures, the doctrines of Karma and transmigration, the quest for deliverance through ritual works and through mystical knowledge, and the ascetic ideal of holiness—these ancient characteristics of Indian religion are still conspicuous and dominant. The two great heresies, Jainism and Buddhism, have not weakened the hold of the Brahmanic system. Jainism has persisted as a relatively small heretical sect. Buddhism, though widespread and influential, has had its main development in other lands; in India, after splitting up into many little sects without much vitality, it has long since suffered its death blow at the hands of an aggressive religion from another land, namely, Mohammedanism.

Meanwhile Brahmanism has gained added strength by the infusion of new blood, so to speak. It has been more or less completely merged with a number of popular religions, thus forming that complicated mixture of ideas and practices which we know as Hinduism. Three ways of salvation are recognized in Hinduism. Brahmanism taught two ways, by works and by knowledge; the popular cults added another, the way of devotion, *i.e.,* the attainment of salvation by trustful and loving devotion to a personal god. Essentially this last conception is the same as the evangelical Christian doctrine of salvation by faith in Christ, though the gods in whom the Hindu trusts are very different from Jesus. The most popular of these gods are Vishnu and Shiva, who are worshipped in countless temples throughout India, with idols and symbols, with offerings and festivals and processions.

By the time of Nanak, as to-day, Hinduism and Mohammedanism were the two chief religions of India. The Mohammedans held the reins of political power for the most part. The influence of the stern monotheistic teaching of Mohammed had already made itself felt in Hinduism in the form of movements for the eradication of polytheism and idolatry. The most important of these reforms was inaugurated in the fifteenth century A.D. by a man named Kabir, to whose teaching several sects in India owe their origin. His followers are known in India to-day as the Kabir Panthis. It would not be altogether inaccurate to call Kabir the Luther of Hinduism, not because of any similarity in their ideas, but because the Kabir Panthis are essentially a Protestant sect within Hinduism.

Even more influential than the teacher was one of his followers, the man with whose life and teaching we are now primarily concerned. As the founder of Jainism drew many of his ideas from earlier monastic orders, so Nanak derived from Kabir much that was most characteristic of his own teaching. The followers of Nanak, however, unlike those of Kabir, formed what is distinctly a separate religion, in the sense that they do not consider themselves Hindus and are not so considered by the adherents of Hinduism. For that reason in our list of the founders of religions we include Nanak but omit Kabir.

The books which tell the story of Nanak's life were written not long after his death. The English scholar who wrote our chief work on Sikhism, as the religion of Nanak is called, used a manuscript which was dated only fifty years later than the year in which Nanak died. This fact might lead us to expect a sober and reliable account of historical events and a clear, trustworthy picture of the personality of Nanak. Instead we find in these books an exuberant growth of legend, with the most fantastic stories of incredible miracles. Evidently legends about the founder of a religion do not require the lapse of centuries for their development. A critical examination of the stories suggests that Nanak's followers read his sayings and used their imaginations in depicting the settings in which the sayings were uttered. Sometimes the personality reflected by the acts attributed to Nanak is quite at variance with that which is expressed in his sayings, just as the apocryphal gospels of the early Christian centuries portray a very different Jesus from the Master who speaks in the pages of the New Testament. The teaching of Nanak is more accurately preserved than the story of his life. The Granth, which is the Bible of Sikhism, was compiled almost a century after Nanak's death, but the materials of which it is composed are considerably earlier, and the sayings and poems of Nanak contained in it were probably handed down with a fair degree of accuracy.

The time in which Nanak lived was the age of the Renaissance and the Reformation in Europe. His birth occurred just before morning on a moonlit night in 1469—not quite a quarter of a century before the discovery of America. Martin Luther was born fourteen years later and died eight years after the death of Nanak; the latter was therefore forty-eight years old when Luther posted his ninety-five theses on the door of the church at Wittenberg.

Celestial music was heard when Nanak was born, it is said. The midwife said that the voice of the newborn babe was that of a wise man, laughing as he joined a social assembly. An astrologer, who came the next day to cast the boy's horoscope, worshipped him. All Nature, he said, as well as both Hindus and Mohammedans, would adore Nanak, who would recognize only one God and would treat God's creatures as creatures. The last statement reminds us, by contrast, of Paul's charge that the Gentiles "worshipped and served the creature rather than the Creator."

Nanak's father was a farmer in a little village in the Punjab. Like the parents of Mahavira and Gautama, he belonged to the second caste, but he was neither a ruler nor a warrior. In addition to his farming he served as village accountant under the feudal lord of the village, a Mohammedan. He was also a merchant in a small way. Nanak's mother was a very devout Hindu woman.

The childhood of Nanak was spent in the ordinary life of farm and village near a great forest. He was a dreamy lad, much given to solitary meditation. At the age of five, according to the books, he was able to converse intelligently about the sacred scriptures of Hinduism. When he was seven years old he was taken to school. The teacher wrote down the alphabet for him, and a day later Nanak wrote it from memory; indeed he composed an acrostic poem in praise of the one God.

Some days later the teacher noticed that Nanak was sitting in silence, not studying his books. He therefore spoke to the boy, but Nanak in reply asked the teacher what he knew. When the teacher said that he knew everything, going on to specify the subjects he had mastered, little Nanak calmly informed him that all such knowledge was worthless. In improvised verse he declared that true knowledge comes only when one makes ink out of the ashes of worldly love, takes faith for his paper, the heart as the pen, and the intellect as the writer, and with these writes the judgment, the True Name and its praises, "that which has no end or limit." Only such knowledge did he care to gain.

The teacher did homage to his precocious pupil, and Nanak withdrew from the school to study and meditate in private, or in the company of holy men. Of course the games of other children had no appeal for such a boy. His favorite associates were the Hindu and Moslem ascetics who dwelt in the forest near his home.

In spite of his contempt for worldly learning, we are told that Nanak learned the Persian language at the age of nine. The local ruler had promised that if he learned this language, which was used for official purposes, he might succeed his father as accountant of the village. As in his earlier study, Nanak composed an acrostic poem on the Persian alphabet, exhorting his teacher to worship the true God. When he was invested with the sacred thread— a Hindu rite corresponding to the Christian ceremony of confirmation—he gave instruction in the same way to the officiating Brahman priest instead of receiving it. While his teaching was of a religious nature, rather than a matter of secular learning, Nanak was evidently by no means an uneducated man. As a matter of fact, as a leading authority on Sikhism has pointed out, the holy men, with whom Nanak as a child consorted in the forest, were proficient in the study of philosophy. Their conversation must have given him an education much more to his taste than that of the village school.

In practical affairs the unworldly boy showed neither interest nor ability. Everything he took out of the house, it is said, he lost. A priest had remarked, when the boy was named, that his fame would be like a canopy over him, but his father, disgusted with his dreamy idleness, said, "A fine canopy!" One day, while watching his father's buffaloes, Nanak fell asleep and allowed them to get into a neighbor's wheat field. Brought before the ruler to answer for the damage done, Nanak claimed that the field had not been injured, and, marvellous to relate, this was found to be true. On a later occasion Nanak again fell asleep while herding buffaloes. The lord of the village, passing by, observed with astonishment that the shadow of the tree under which Nanak lay had not moved as the day advanced but stood still over the young saint.

As he grew older Nanak became no more competent in practical matters. One day, when he was twelve years old, his father said to him in despair, "You have disgraced me." Nanak made no reply, and the broken-hearted man cried out, "I am worn out and dying, and you say never a word." Even at the age of seventeen the boy was a sore trial to his father. Sent out one day with twenty rupees to trade, he set forth with many promises and (we may believe) with the best of intentions. Meeting a company of religious devotees, however, he bestowed the money upon them and returned home empty-handed. His angry father struck him on both cheeks.

Both of Nanak's parents endeavored to lead him into some profitable occupation. When his father urged him to take up farming, Nanak replied with a poem on spiritual husbandry. The suggestion that he become a storekeeper met with a similar response, as did also a third proposal, that he engage in horse-trading. The family and neighbors at last came to the conclusion that Nanak was mad, and sent for a physician to see if anything could be done for him. When the physician felt his pulse, Nanak laughed and spoke in verse, as was his wont. "Physician," he said, "go home; few know my malady. The Creator, who gave me this pain, will remove it." Asked by the physician to describe his own malady, Nanak again expressed himself at length in verse, declaring that his pain was the pain of separation from God. Hearing this, the physician announced that Nanak was in good health, paid homage to him, and departed.

Meanwhile, when only fourteen years old, Nanak had been married. The union was not a happy one. We have no reason to find fault with Nanak's wife. She had married a saint, and saints are notoriously hard to live with. Perhaps also, as has been suggested, some weight must be given to the fact that the marriage, in accordance with Hindu usage, had been arranged by the parents of the young couple. Left to himself, Nanak probably would not have married at all. Family responsibilities made no change in him. Two sons were born, but still he spent most of his time in retirement and meditation. At last his parents in despair sent him to another town, where his married sister lived. His wife begged to be taken with him, declaring that when he was with her she felt as though she were queen of the earth. Nanak, however, said that he was of no use to her, and that he would send for her if he was able to make a living. The local ruler, who regarded Nanak as a very superior being, gave a banquet in his honor before the saint departed for his new home.

A position as storekeeper under the government was secured for him by his sister's husband. Contrary to what one might expect, Nanak was efficient and successful in this occupation. He supported himself and had money to give to holy men, though we do not read that he sent any home to his wife or that he ever sent for her to join him. Even in his business his piety was still manifest. The word meaning *thirteen* in the language of that country means also *thine*, and whenever Nanak reached this number in weighing or counting, he used to repeat the word again and again—"Thine, Thine, Thine"—exactly in the sense of the Christian hymn, "I am Thine, O Lord."

A musician named Mardana, a Mohammedan, now came from Nanak's home village and lived with him as his servant. Others also of his former neighbors joined him, and he secured employment for them with the ruler of the district. Every evening the friends met with Nanak and sang together. Nanak sang them songs of his own composition, while Mardana accompanied him on what Milton calls "the jocund rebeck."

Yet Nanak was not happy. His soul was athirst for God; he could neither eat nor drink, so sick was he with unsatisfied longing. One morning, taking his customary bath in the river, he stayed in the water longer than usual. Some think he fell into a trance while in the water; others say that he came out of the river and went into the forest. At any rate the experience which his heart desired was granted to him. In a vision he entered into the presence of God, who said to him, "I am with thee. I have made thee happy, and also those who shall take thy name. Go and repeat Mine, and cause others to do likewise. Abide uncontaminated by the world. Practise the repetition of My name, charity, ablutions, worship, and meditation. I have given thee this cup of nectar, a pledge of my regard." Nanak arose, made obeisance, and sang a spontaneous psalm of adoration, accompanied by celestial strains of music. The hymn ended with these lines:

"Had I thousands of thousands of tons of paper and a desire
    to write on it all after the deepest research;
  Were ink never to fail me, and could I move my pen like the
    wind,
  I should still not be able to express Thy worth; how great
    shall I call Thy Name?"

For three days Nanak remained in the forest; then, obedient to the heavenly vision, he went back to his house and gave away everything he had. The people of the village thought he was possessed and sent for a Moslem priest to drive out the demon. Nanak's remarks during the process of exorcism convinced them that he was not possessed but insane. Commanding Mardana to play on his rebeck, Nanak then sang a song ending thus:

"When a man loveth the Lord and deemeth himself worthless
And the rest of the world good, he is called mad."

Assuming the scanty garb of the ascetic, Nanak now frequented more than ever the company of holy men. One day, after sitting in silence throughout the day preceding, he uttered the startling declaration, "There is no Hindu and no Moslem!" He was commanded to appear before the ruler and explain his statement, but he refused to go. Summoned a second time, he presented himself before the ruler, who expressed disappointment that so capable an official should devote himself to the ascetic life. Being a Mohammedan, the ruler had at his court an official expounder of the Mohammedan laws, whom he now directed to question Nanak regarding the meaning of the enigmatic statement, "There is no Hindu and no Moslem." Nanak answered the questions in verse to the accompaniment of Mardana's rebeck. The import of his replies may be seen from the following lines:

"To be a Moslem is difficult: If one be really so, then one may
be called a Moslem.

. . . .

Make kindness thy mosque, sincerity thy prayer-carpet, what
is just and lawful thy Koran.

. . . .

If thou make good works the creed thou repeatest, thou shalt
be a Moslem."

When the time came for the regular afternoon prayer, Nanak went with the rest into the mosque, but as the service began he laughed aloud. At the close of the service an explanation of his irreverent conduct was demanded. Nanak said that the leader, while praying with his lips, was worrying about a little colt, which he feared might fall into an open well; and the ruler, outwardly participating in worship, had his mind on horse-trading all the time. On that account the prayers were not acceptable to God; hence Nanak's derisive laughter. The listening Moslems were astonished at these statements and besought Nanak to teach them the true religion. He responded with a hymn which moved the ruler to fall at his feet and offer him wealth and power. Nanak declined these gifts and once more betook himself to the forest.

Two unpleasant episodes in connection with his work finally drove him to devote himself exclusively to the religious life. He was twice accused of misappropriating money belonging to the government. On both occasions he was vindicated; indeed it was found that the government owed him money, which at his request was given to the poor. But the experience added the last drop to his disgust with the world. After a brief period of retirement in the forest, he emerged and began a protracted period of itinerant evangelism. He was now a Guru (Teacher). Taking Mardana with him, he travelled all over northern India, preaching and singing the gospel of an inclusive faith which sought to combine the truth of both Hinduism and Islam. To symbolize the eclectic character of his message he adopted a motley costume in which the characteristic features of both Moslem and Hindu dress were combined. He did not hesitate, however, to attack what he considered false in both religions, and his preaching alienated many who heard him. Like Gautama, he abandoned his earlier asceticism, and this too offended many people. The Brahmans were horrified by his eating meat. Nevertheless great crowds assembled to hear him wherever he went.

With the energy of a Paul or a Wesley, Nanak went from one place of pilgrimage to another. Perilous adventures were sometimes encountered, but he always emerged victorious. A wicked robber, who pretended to be very hospitable and very religious, but murdered his guests as they slept, received the two evangelists, but on hearing the hymn which Nanak recited when retiring for the night he abandoned his treacherous designs against them and became a Sikh (Disciple). After making restitution for his crimes, he received the rite which in Sikhism takes the place held by baptism in Christianity. The central element in this rite consists of drinking water in which the Guru's feet have been washed.

At a religious fair Nanak made many converts. At another sacred place, where throngs had gathered to wash their sins away, he attracted attention by an act which recalls the dramatic methods of the Hebrew prophets. Seeing a group of pilgrims throwing water toward the east, he threw water toward the west. A crowd assembled about him. When the people asked him why he threw water toward the west, he asked them why they were throwing it toward the east. They said it was for the shades of their ancestors. He asked how far away the shades were and was told that they were thousands of miles away. Then he silently resumed his eccentric action, until the people pressed him for an explanation. He solemnly informed them that he was irrigating a field which would dry up if not thus supplied with water. The people called him a fool, but he replied, "My field, which you say this water cannot reach, is near, but your ancestors are very far away, so how could the water ye offer them ever reach them or profit them?"

After travelling extensively through northern India, Nanak turned his face to the east. Still he was beset by many perils. Once he was attacked by brigands. He instructed them to devote their plunder to charity and take up farming, which they forthwith proceeded to do. Many converts were made among both Hindus and Mohammedans. A group of women renowned for sorcery was induced to give up the black art. Not least among Nanak's triumphs was his victory over the Evil One, who tempted him to relinquish his work, offering him wealth, women, and world-wide power.

Returning from eastern India, Nanak and Mardana again journeyed through the northern districts, then turned once more to the east. Many friends were made and disciples added to the Guru's following, but persecution and hardship were encountered also. Mardana, apparently of somewhat less robust piety than Nanak, suffered so from hunger that sometimes he could not sing or play. After twelve years of loyal devotion, he begged Nanak to let him go home. Nanak finally returned with him. The friends and relatives of both received them with joy. Nanak's mother and father came out of the village to meet him. He greeted them respectfully and gladly but would not yield to their entreaties that he come into the village and take up his abode with them again. Apparently he did not see his wife at all.

Almost immediately he set out again, and again the faithful Mardana went with him. The second missionary journey was even longer than the first. Some of the territory traversed before was revisited, and old friendships were renewed. In one village there was no one who would show hospitality to the Guru except a leper. Nanak lodged with the wretched creature and healed his loathsome disease. During this journey Nanak saw a city laid waste by the cruel Mogul emperor, Baber. The Guru himself and his attendant were imprisoned by the invaders and put to hard labor. Their work, however, was miraculously done for them, and the emperor perceived that his prisoners were holy men. They were therefore released, and at Nanak's request the other captives from the city were given their liberty also. The suffering of the people during this bloody time impressed Nanak profoundly. In one of his hymns he cries, "When there was such slaughter and lamentation, didst not Thou, O God, feel pain?"

For some time Nanak made his headquarters on the banks of the Ravi River, where a local magnate founded a new village in his honor. Societies of Sikhs were organized, a temple was built, and a regular order of daily worship was established, consisting principally of the reading and singing of Nanak's hymns. A common meal of all the disciples in the evening was a part of the daily programme. Nanak spent his time in prayer and teaching. Meditation and singing were emphasized in contrast to the formal acts of Hindu ritual.

One of Nanak's followers made a commercial voyage to Ceylon and there spread the fame of the Guru. A little later Nanak journeyed with some of his followers to the southern part of India. Here he is said to have converted a Jain priest by a bitter satire on Jainism—an achievement indeed, for satire is not usually an effective means of conversion. Many other places were visited and many other remarkable conversions made. Nanak even reached Ceylon and preached to the king and queen there. Returning to India, he went to a religious fair and debated with the priests, confounding the expounders of all the six great schools of Hindu philosophy. To an invitation to drink wine with some of them he responded with a poem exalting the intoxication of communion with God. "Why should he who dealeth in nectar," he said, "feel love for paltry wine?"

Turning north again, Nanak traversed the entire length of the peninsula and ascended the peaks of the Himalayas, where he was received and honored by a company of holy men. He then turned west and visited many great centres of the Mohammedan religion. In the guise of a Moslem pilgrim he even visited Mecca, we are told. Here he lay down to sleep with his feet turned toward the Kaaba. A Mohammedan priest reproached him for "turning his feet toward God." "Show me," said Nanak, "how I may turn my feet where God is not." The Moslem then forcibly turned Nanak's feet away from the Kaaba, whereupon it left its place and moved to a position in front of him. Not only Mecca but Medina and Baghdad also were included in the amazing itinerary, and the Mohammedan leaders in these cities were overcome by Nanak in debate.

When one of them asked him to what sect he belonged, he replied, "I reject all sects and only know one God."

After this Nanak returned to the village which had been established for him and his followers. Here the loyal Mardana died. At last, when his own end drew near, Nanak appointed one of his disciples to succeed him. His sons could not carry on his work, for they were insincere and disobedient and had deserted him, we are told, and we can hardly wonder at this when we recall what a father he had been to them. In October, 1538, the end came to the Guru in a most marvellous and significant way. Perceiving that their teacher was about to die, his followers disputed about the proper way to dispose of his remains. Those who had been converted from Hinduism said he should be cremated; those who had come from Mohammedanism were in favor of burial. Nanak decided the matter by directing that the Hindus should leave flowers beside him on his right side and the Moslems on his left, and that they whose flowers should be found blooming in the morning should dispose of his body. After saying this he covered himself with a sheet. In the morning it was found that both the Hindus' and the Mohammedans' flowers were blooming, but there was nothing under the sheet.

Nanak belongs distinctly to the group described by William James as the "twice born," those who have suffered from sickness of soul, and whose divided selves have been fused into unity by a decisive spiritual experience. Before his vision of God Nanak was unhappy and unwell. His unworldliness and his utter lack of practical efficiency or even reliability, however trying they must have been to his family and friends, bespeak an earnest preoccupation with the things of the spirit. The sayings preserved in the Granth express a deep and wretched sense of sinfulness. "I am not chaste, nor truthful, nor learned," says the unhappy Nanak in one passage; "foolish and ignorant am I." To infer from this that he was ever actually unchaste or untruthful would be as unwarranted as to draw the same conclusion from the apostle Paul's complaint, "For the good that I would I do not, but the evil which I would not that I do." Before his conversion Paul felt that he was "carnal, sold under sin," though it is said elsewhere that his life was blameless according to the strictest rules of the Pharisees. So Nanak may have lived an exemplary life even while his acutely sensitive conscience convicted him of sin. His statement, "I am a cheat in a country of cheats," calls to mind the cry of the prophet Isaiah, "I am a man of unclean lips, and I dwell in the midst of a people of unclean lips." And it is clearly an earnest seeker after God who says, "I am a sinner, Thou alone art pure," just as Charles Wesley wrote, "Vile and full of sin I am; Thou art full of truth and grace." Nanak's attainment of happy assurance after a period of unhappy groping recalls the experiences of Mohammed and Gautama.

In other respects also Nanak reminds us of Buddha. He does not seem to have had Gautama's understanding and consideration for others, nor, perhaps, his surpassing intellectual power and originality, though the evidence in our hands is hardly sufficient for a just decision in these matters. Both Gautama and Nanak, however, rejected asceticism after trying it. Both were superior to the common tendency toward fanatical devotion to extreme positions. Both won the devoted affection of their followers, for while Nanak's relations with his own family were not altogether happy, it is clear that his disciples not only admired him but loved him. Their favorite name for him was Baba Nanak, *i.e.,* Papa Nanak. Like Gautama, again, Nanak has been deified by his followers. It is even said that during his lifetime people addressed him as a god and asked him to forgive their sins and save them. No abstruse doctrines regarding his divinity have been developed, as in Buddhism and Christianity, but he is adored as divine and identified with Brahma. In certain minor and external features, also, there is some similarity between the lives of Nanak and Buddha, yet the comparison must not be pressed too far, for the differences are as great as the resemblances.

Certainly their teachings were not much alike. Indeed, while Nanak's sayings evince no great originality, the very fact that they combine ideas from religions as dissimilar as Hinduism and Mohammedanism makes them different from anything else that we have found. The religion of the Sikhs, or Disciples, is unique among the religions of the world in having originated as a deliberate attempt to combine two other religions. The environment of Nanak's childhood had given him a first-hand acquaintance with both Hinduism and Islam. The example of Mohammedanism, together with the influence of Kabir, made him dissatisfied with polytheism, idolatry, ritualism, and the caste system. Of the two roots of his teaching, however, Hinduism was the more influential. With all his appreciation of some aspects of the Arabian faith, Nanak remained a true child of India. This is at once evident in his conception of God. True, a strong and consistent em-

phasis upon the unity and the sovereignty of God evinces
the influence of Mohammedanism, and many expressions
in the Granth might almost have been taken word for word
from the Koran: "Like Thee there is no other," "Thou hast
no partner who is brought near," "He is King, the King of
kings. All remain subject to His will," "What is pleasure to
Thee, that exists." Mohammedan as well as Hindu names
for God are used in the Granth, though Nanak's favorite
designation for the Deity is simply "the True Name."
But the God of Nanak is not Allah; in his essential nature
he is still the Hindu Brahma, a personal Being yet retaining also some of the characteristics of the Absolute Reality
as conceived by the ancient philosophers—one, indivisible,
indescribable. In other words, Nanak's monotheism approaches monism or pantheism, in which God not only is
over all, but *is* the All.

Accordingly Nanak's idea of salvation is more Hindu
than Mohammedan. The goal of his endeavor and aspiration is not acquittal in the judgment on the day of resurrection, followed by the enjoyment of Paradise, but realization of the unreality of individual existence and complete
absorption in Brahma, the One Reality. Nanak's Hindu
heritage was too strong to let him substitute resurrection
and judgment for transmigration and Karma, or Paradise
for deliverance from rebirth and union with Brahma. During one of his peregrinations with Mardana a great man
was seen sitting in the shade of a tree and being shampooed
and fanned by perspiring servants. This spectacle of social
inequality moved Mardana to ask whether the rich did not
have one God and the poor another. In reply Nanak told
him, in true Hindu fashion, that the fortunes and misfor-

tunes of this life were the result of men's deeds in former incarnations.

At the same time Nanak taught that the wicked would be punished in hell—an idea, of course, not new or unfamiliar in Indian religion. Banishment from God's presence is mentioned as the punishment of the unrighteous. The Granth says also that they will "sit outside weeping," just as Jesus spoke of the "outer darkness," where would be "weeping and gnashing of teeth." One of Nanak's hymns specifies many horrible forms of infernal retribution along with the doom of repeated transmigration.

Nanak's way of obtaining salvation, like his conception of the meaning of salvation, is characteristically Indian. The old reliance upon ritual works is entirely abandoned; a certain degree of merit is attached to ceremonial observances, but there are no sacrifices, and salvation cannot be attained by the performance of any rite. The external trappings of religion had no appeal for Nanak. Once, when invited to take part in the elaborate ceremonial worship of a Hindu temple, he raised his eyes to heaven instead and chanted,

"The sun and moon, O Lord, are Thy lamps; the firmament Thy salver; the orbs of the stars the pearls enchased in it.

The perfume of the sandal is Thine incense; the wind is Thy fan; all the forests are Thy flowers, O Lord of light."

Possibly Mohammedan influence had something to do with this departure from the ancient system, yet there had been abundant precedents for it in many native religious movements. The influence of Islam appears more directly in the conception of submission to the eternal and omnipotent will of God, which is expressed in the Granth in true Mohammedan fashion. Even the doctrine of predestination is implied, if not declared explicitly. "What pleaseth God will happen. There is nothing whatever in the power of his creatures." "It is God who causeth to act, and who acteth himself." Even here, however, if one does not analyze the ideas too minutely, it is clear that Moslem and Hindu beliefs have been fused. Submission to a heavenly Potentate is not the same as the merging of individual personality with the Self of the universe, but Nanak probably regarded the two conceptions as essentially identical. The spiritual experience was more important for him than its theological definition, and he was probably content to let Mohammedans describe it in one way and Hindus in another.

None the less his view of the way of salvation is more like the Brahman way of mystical knowledge than the Mohammedan way of submission to Allah, and it is still more closely related to the way of devotion practised by the cults of Vishnu and Shiva. In the devout piety of his mother Nanak had seen what devotion to Vishnu might mean, and it was in this passionate personal love for God that he found the true way of salvation. Often in the Granth the bliss of union with God is expressed in the ardent language of human love. Moslem as well as Hindu mystics had often used the same form of expression, just as Christian mystics have found in the amorous poesy of the Song of Solomon a fitting vehicle for their spiritual rapture. Mysticism is not peculiar to any one religion, but the doctrine of salvation by devotion as preached by Nanak was taken over directly from Hinduism, and in particular from the worship of Vishnu.

In one respect, however, Nanak's dependence upon either Hinduism or Islam is not so obvious, though no less real in fact. While man is saved by grace through faith, Nanak did not teach that faith is by itself sufficient for the attainment of salvation. As the Catholic Church maintains that God's saving grace can be received only by taking the sacraments at the hands of a duly ordained priest, so Nanak taught that the believer is dependent upon the mediation of the Guru, *i.e.*, Nanak himself or his direct successor. The Guru, says the Granth, is a boat which conveys man across the dangerous ocean of existence by the Name of the Lord; he is the ladder by which man ascends into the palace of the Lord. When the Guru sees in a believer the evidence of the divine choice, he conveys to him God's saving grace by the recitation of a mystic formula. This doctrine of dependence upon the Teacher is not a prominent characteristic of either Hinduism or Islam, but it was not without precedent in both religions. It had been especially stressed by Nanak's immediate predecessor, Kabir, from whom Nanak doubtless received it.

While the grace of God is appropriated by loving devotion, a righteous life also is required of Nanak's followers. "At the throne of God," he once said, "grace is obtained by two things: open confession and reparation for wrong." When the sorceresses to whom he preached during one of his missionary journeys asked him what they should do to be saved, he prescribed a conscientious performance of their household duties along with the repetition of the Name and the renunciation of magic. One of Nanak's hymns contrasts the outward observances of religion with its true substance in a way which recalls both the prophets of the

Old Testament and the familiar definition of "pure religion and undefiled" in the Epistle of James. The following quotation is typical:

"Religion consisteth not in wandering in foreign countries, or in bathing at places of pilgrimages. Abide pure amid the impurities of the world; thus shalt thou find the way of religion."

Sikhism rejects the caste system and accords a higher position to woman than she enjoys in either Hinduism or Islam. Asceticism is repudiated even more completely than in Mohammedanism, which has its month of fasting every year. Yet Nanak did not, with some Hindu sects, encourage self-indulgence. Some of his sayings recall what Paul wrote about dying to sin. Sikhs, like Moslems, are forbidden the use of wine; the strictest of them to-day abjure also tobacco, which of course was not known in India in Nanak's day. In sharp contrast to the Hindus, the Sikhs are meat-eaters—and therefore much larger and stronger in body than the other peoples of India. In his ethical teaching Nanak is far more Moslem than Hindu. Hinduism is inclined to distinguish rather sharply between morality and religion, though it is by no means true that the religion is without ethical standards. In this as in other respects there are great differences between the various forms of Hinduism. In renouncing asceticism and teaching that salvation is to be sought in the common walks of life, instead of by withdrawal from the world, Nanak resembles Zoroaster as well as Mohammed. Unlike these two, however, he agreed with Lao-tze and Jesus in holding that evil should be repaid with good: "if a man beat thee, strike him not in return, but stoop and kiss his feet." The passage from which this is quoted is recited daily by the Sikhs and is said to affect their conduct marvellously.

Nanak gave the Sikhs not only a faith but also an organization, which is known as the Pure Congregation. Like Jainism, the religion owes its permanence in part to the strength of its organization. Membership is voluntary: to this day a man is a Sikh not by birth but by choice. One member of a family may be a Sikh while another is a Hindu. Herein Sikhism has not gone the way of Jainism and Zoroastrianism. Under Nanak and his immediate successors the congregation was not concerned with political power, but the authority of the Gurus tended to convert the religious organization into an independent community, and within a century after Nanak's death the Sikhs had become a nation. Nanak himself was not, like Mohammed, a secular ruler as well as a religious leader, but his later successors were. As "the Lions of the Punjab" the Sikhs became famous soldiers. It is said that the demand for Sikhs in the British army to-day brings many converts to the religion. Since the middle of the nineteenth century, however, when their last ruler surrendered to Queen Victoria, the Sikhs have had no political independence. As in Judaism and Mohammedanism, what was once a nation is now purely a religion; in this case, however, the change is a return to the original intention of the founder.

Numerically Sikhism is not strong to-day, and it has not spread appreciably beyond its original home, the Punjab. Among the eleven living religions of the world it is the ninth in size, though it is three times as large as Jainism and thirty times as large as Zoroastrianism. Once more it is not the number of his followers that measures the importance of Nanak. By no standard, perhaps, would he be counted among the greatest of the founders we are studying. One fact, however, is well worth pointing out: evangelistic zeal is rarely combined in the same individual, as it was in Nanak, with a sympathetic appreciation of more than one religion.

CHAPTER TEN

JESUS

FRIEND OF SINNERS AND BRINGER OF GOOD NEWS

To speak of the founder of one's own religion exactly as
one speaks of the founders of other religions is extremely
difficult, if not impossible. The very attempt to do it causes
something of a pang: it seems, somehow, disloyal. Yet it
must be attempted; otherwise we can have no fair basis for
comparison. Since our object is not to prove that one religion or one founder is better than another, but simply to
find what they have in common and wherein they differ,
we must consider them all from the same point of view.
The purpose of this chapter is to review the life and teaching of Jesus in such a way as to make a just comparison
possible.

This means, among other things, that we must speak of
Jesus as a man like other men. To our personal faith he
may be more than that, but we have seen that the founders
of almost all religions are regarded by their followers as in
some sense divine. Since we have been considering them
purely as men, and could not consider them in any other
light, we must for our present purpose regard our Lord too
as a human teacher. We must make our study as objective
and as impartial as human nature will allow us to make it.
If we cannot thus secure a picture of Jesus which would

fully satisfy all Christians, we must remember that our pictures of the other founders would not satisfy their followers either. At least we shall have some common ground, some basis for comparison which people of all faiths may accept as being true as far as it goes.

Jesus was born about 6 B.C., "in the days of Herod the king." The familiar Christmas story hardly needs to be repeated here. All Christians are acquainted with Matthew's account of Joseph's dream, in which an angel told him that his betrothed, Mary, though still a virgin, was to bring forth a son by the power of the Holy Spirit, and that this son would "save his people from their sins"; then the birth in Bethlehem, the visit of the wise men from the east following the star, the flight of Joseph and Mary with the babe into Egypt to escape Herod's slaughter of the children in Bethlehem, their return after Herod's death, and their settling in Nazareth. Equally familiar is Luke's story of the birth of John the Baptist, the journey of Joseph and Mary to Bethlehem to be enrolled, the birth of Jesus in a stable because of the crowded condition of the inn, the appearance of the angels to the shepherds, the circumcision of Jesus, and his presentation in the temple. Both Matthew and Luke trace the descent of Joseph, though by different lines, to David, from whose seed the promised Messiah was to come.

We know very little of Jesus' childhood. The late apocryphal gospels tell many fantastic tales. One of these, which is referred to in the Koran, relates that Jesus in boyish sport made a bird out of mud and then gave it life, so that it flew away. Many miracles of healing and raising the dead, and also instances of cursing people, who immediately fainted or fell dead, are given in these curious documents of early Christianity. Only one incident of Jesus' boyhood, however, is narrated in the New Testament. Luke tells us that when Jesus was twelve years old he attended the Passover with his parents in Jerusalem. Inadvertently left behind when the caravan set out for home, he was found after three days in the temple, astonishing the learned scribes with his penetrating questions and answers. From Joseph Jesus learned the carpenter's trade, and it seems probable that the death of Joseph threw upon Jesus in his early manhood the responsibility of supporting his mother and his younger brothers and sisters.

The circumstances under which Jesus grew to manhood were quite different from those which we have found in the case of any other founder. The Jews at the beginning of our era were living in rebellious discontent under the domination of the Roman Empire. After being ruled for centuries by Babylonians, Persians, and Greeks in turn, they had been free from foreign control for about a hundred years, but the independent Maccabean dynasty had quickly degenerated, and more than half a century before the birth of Jesus the Romans had become the masters of Palestine as they were of the surrounding countries. King Herod, strong as he was, maintained his power only by assiduously playing the sycophant, first to Cassius of the "lean and hungry look," then to Mark Antony and Augustus in turn as each gained the upper hand. Not long after the birth of Jesus Herod died, and his kingdom was divided among his sons. The one who inherited Judea was deposed for disloyalty to Rome in 6 A.D., and his territory was governed by Roman procurators during Jesus' lifetime, but Galilee and the country east of the Jordan remained in the hands of Herod's sons for a number of years after the death of Jesus.

Herod was not of Jewish extraction, and he and his sons were not much loved by the Jews. Nor were the Romans held in affectionate esteem. There was much unrest among the people. A serious uprising against the government took place not long after the time of Jesus' birth, and another when he was about twelve years old. Disorder and brigandage were rife in the land. Some of the Jews were in favor of armed revolt; others counselled submission and quiet trust in God for deliverance and vengeance. No one was satisfied, except the hated publicans, who took advantage of the Roman system of taxation to fatten themselves on the substance of their countrymen. Affairs were moving rapidly toward the terrible rebellion of 66–70 A.D. and the destruction of the temple, which some of Jesus' immediate followers lived to see.

Such political conditions could not fail to have an effect upon religious life and thought. Patriotism and religion have always been closely bound together in Judaism. Since the days of the great prophets the Jews had hoped for the coming of the Lord's Anointed, a descendant of the royal line of David who should sit upon the throne of Judah and restore the ancient glories of the monarchy. The term Messiah, of which the word Christ is the literal equivalent in Greek, means *Anointed*. It is the word applied in the Old Testament to King Saul and his successors. The Messianic hope was primarily a hope of restored political independence and power. Since the Babylonian exile, however, centuries of disappointment had caused the Jews to turn to another kind of hope, patterned after ideas which were current in Zoroastrianism and other faiths of the peoples among whom the Jews were living. Not merely political restoration by the help of God, but a miraculous divine intervention and the inauguration of God's own Heavenly Kingdom; not merely the deliverance of the nation as a whole, but the resurrection of the righteous dead to take part in the life of the Kingdom; not merely a human descendant of David, but a divine Son of Man, who would come in glory on the clouds of heaven—these were the outstanding features of what is called the apocalyptic hope, which grew ever brighter as the Jews suffered more and more at the hands of their foreign rulers. Some of the people still held to the old prophetic hope of a Davidic Messiah; some preferred the newer apocalyptic vision; many doubtless combined and confused them. In one form or another, both among those who wished to "seize the kingdom of Heaven by violence" and among those who had faith to "wait patiently for the Lord," the hope of a great deliverance was seething and boiling in the heart of the nation.

Officially the religion of the Jews still centred in the temple, which Herod had enlarged and enriched. Here the large and highly organized class of priests and Levites carried on the solemn pageantry of the sacrificial cultus, with prescribed offerings for every morning and evening and special observances for all the days of feasting or fasting. For more than a century and a half the office of the high priest had been treated by the ruling powers as a matter of political spoil and had thus passed from one unworthy incumbent to another. The priests, as a class, belonged to the aristocratic party known as the Sadducees. Theologically conservative, in that they rejected the relatively new beliefs regarding angels and the resurrection, they were inclined to laxity as regards social customs, taking up with considerable enthusiasm the ways of their Greek and Roman masters in place of the strict and exclusive usages of traditional Judaism. In spite of political corruption and social cosmopolitanism, however, the priests were still the official representatives of the religion of Israel, and the nation's loyalty had its focus in the temple and its services.

The chief exponents of social conservatism were the Pharisees, a sect which had grown out of resistance to foreign innovations and devotion to the traditions of the fathers. The beliefs in the resurrection and in the world of angels, which had developed in connection with the apocalyptic hopes described above, were cherished by the Pharisees as though they were an essential part of the old religion. The chief object of their devotion, however, was the Law, including both the written Law of the Old Testament and the oral traditions which interpreted and applied it. So extensive and involved had these traditions become that a class of professional experts, the scribes, had arisen. The "people of the land," as the common people were called, not having the leisure to become acquainted with the vast system of traditional law, were less strict in their observance of the Law than were the wealthy and respectable Pharisees. In a sense the Pharisees were the Puritans of Judaism, and with them, as elsewhere, the Puritan disposition often produced a sort of spiritual pride and self-satisfaction, which was sometimes carried to the point of downright hypocrisy. The unlovely qualities which

we designate as Pharisaic, however, cannot be fairly predicated of the Pharisees as a whole. The primary characteristic of the Pharisees was their devotion—narrow, perhaps, but thoroughly sincere—to the Law and its traditional
interpretation.

Another important feature of the Judaism of Jesus' day
must be kept in mind if we would understand his life and
teaching. The sacrificial rites of the temple did not constitute the only worship of God, nor were the common
people left in utter ignorance of the Law. Domestic observances and the instruction of the young by their parents
were important then as now; also the people assembled in
the local synagogues three times a week, including the Sabbath, for prayer and the reading and interpretation of the
Scriptures. Since Hebrew was no longer the language of
the people, the Scripture Lessons were not only read in the
original but also translated into Aramaic, so that all might
understand them.

There was not, as at present, a regular rabbi, elected and
paid by the congregation. If the title "rabbi" was used at all
in the time of Jesus, it was applied to the authorized teachers of the Law. These were appointed by the Sanhedrin,
the council of elders in Jerusalem. Of course if such a rabbi
happened to be present in the synagogue he would be asked
to take part in the service, but his presence was not necessary. Any man who was known as a religious leader might
be asked to speak, as both Jesus and Paul are said to have
been on various occasions.

In addition to the synagogue there were many schools,
in which boys were given elementary instruction in the
Scriptures. Higher schools existed also for more advanced

study of the Law. Thus the fundamental principles of the religion were instilled into the people as a whole, while the subtle intricacies of the traditional interpretation and application of the Law were passed on and increasingly elaborated by the scribes and rabbis and their disciples.

Such was the spiritual environment of Jesus' youth and early manhood. Political unrest, Messianic and apocalyptic hopes, the imposing ceremonial of the temple, the divergent views and customs of Sadducees and Pharisees, the learned legalism of the scribes and the simple piety of the "people of the land," the general acquaintance with the Scriptures through home and school and synagogue—all these were, so to speak, familiar features of his spiritual landscape.

When Jesus was about thirty years old, an ardent herald of God's Kingdom appeared in the person of John the Baptist, so called because he baptized in the Jordan River those who by repentance had prepared themselves for the approaching day of the Lord. John was a stern messenger of judgment like the Old Testament prophets. In garb and manner he especially resembled Elijah, and the early Christians saw in him a fulfilment of the words of Scripture: "Behold, I will send you Elijah the prophet before the coming of the great and terrible day of the Lord"; "Behold, I send my messenger before thy face"; "The voice of one crying in the wilderness, Prepare ye the way of the Lord."

Recent research has made it evident that John was a greater figure than we had supposed. He did not only prepare the way for Jesus; he initiated an independent religious movement which continued to exist alongside of Christianity for some time. The strange sect of the Mandæans, who to-day claim to be the followers of John the Baptist, may not go back to him directly, but it is evident from the New Testament itself that John's movement was not at once absorbed by Christianity.

Luke tells us that the mothers of John and Jesus were related, but there is no evidence that the two men ever saw each other before Jesus came to hear John preach and was baptized at his hands in the Jordan. By receiving this rite Jesus identified himself with the movement which John had inaugurated. The gospels say that John had foretold the coming of one much greater than himself, and that he recognized in Jesus the one who was to come. Later, however, when in prison, he sent some of his followers to Jesus to ask, "Art thou he that should come, or do we look for another?"

To Jesus himself the baptism in the Jordan was undoubtedly the occasion of a great spiritual experience. "And straightway coming up out of the water, he saw the heavens opened and the Spirit like a dove descending upon him; and there came a voice from heaven saying, Thou art my beloved Son, in whom I am well pleased." Whether this was the first dawning in Jesus' mind of a sense of special relationship to God, or whether it simply confirmed what he had already come to believe, we cannot tell. Certainly it marks the beginning of his special religious mission.

Immediately following it came a preparatory period of trial in the solitude of the desert. Here Jesus faced the problems of the work he felt called to undertake and the various ways of doing it that lay open to him. The gospels tell of this temptation in the form of a conversation between Jesus and Satan. Since there were no witnesses,

Jesus must have told the disciples about it himself, and doubtless he described in this form the inner struggle through which the nature of his mission had become clear to him. How long after this he began his public work is unknown. We are told simply that after John the Baptist was thrown into prison Jesus appeared in Galilee, proclaiming the nearness of the Kingdom, as John had done, and calling upon the people to repent.

It is impossible to give a chronological outline of Jesus' ministry. Many writers have traced three years of public activity: a year of obscurity, a year of popularity, and a year of opposition. This scheme, however, depends upon unwarranted assumptions. The gospels were written within a few decades after Jesus' death and make use of still earlier materials, but they are spiritual interpretations of Jesus, not biographies in the strict sense of the word. Their contents are not arranged chronologically but topically: for example a group of selected parables shows Jesus as a teacher, a group of miracles presents him as a healer, while another group of incidents gives typical cases of controversy with his opponents. As regards the order of events, therefore, we can only say that Jesus' activity centred at first in Galilee, especially in and about the city of Capernaum at the head of the Sea of Galilee, and that it ended in Jerusalem.

In the synagogues, on the seashore, and on country hillsides Jesus proclaimed his message, "and the common people heard him gladly." "And all bare him witness and wondered at the gracious words which proceeded out of his mouth." He became widely known also as a marvellous healer of diseases, and the afflicted flocked to him seeking relief. Many followers joined him and went about with him from place to place. Twelve of them were chosen as an especially intimate circle, "that they might be with him, and that he might send them forth to preach and to have authority to cast out demons."

Not everybody, however, was pleased with his teaching. His old neighbors in Nazareth had no faith in him. Even his own family thought him insane and tried to restrain him. More serious for his work was the opposition of the religious leaders of the nation, who felt that his teaching and the example which he set before the people were subversive of true religion. His free association with the lowest dregs of society and his indifference to many of the accepted requirements of the legal traditions offended these leaders; doubtless also his very popularity aroused some fear of political complications, for the Romans would hold them responsible for anything that looked like sedition, and recent Messianic movements had made them wary of allowing any leader of the people to become too influential.

Apparently it became evident to Jesus at length that the nation as a whole would not accept his call to repentance and faith in the approaching Kingdom; indeed the gospels represent him as foreseeing clearly that his work would eventuate in rejection and death. Yet as the Passover season drew near, when Jews from far and near would assemble in the holy city, "he steadfastly set his face to go to Jerusalem." Some scholars believe that he intended at this time to present himself publicly as the promised Son of David and hoped that the nation would rally to him. Whether that is true or not can only be a matter of conjecture. If we cannot clearly trace the outward course of events, still less can we follow the development of Jesus' inner thoughts and purposes.

Whatever he may have intended or hoped, he appeared in the temple and taught the people as he had taught them in Galilee. Finding that the money-changers had made the temple "a den of thieves" instead of "a house of prayer," he violently drove them from the house of God. At night he withdrew to the nearby village of Bethany or to the Mount of Olives. The authorities did not dare to apprehend him openly, beeause many of the people looked upon him as a prophet, and their resentment would have increased the unrest which the rulers wished to allay. One of his own disciples, however, through greed or through disappointment that Jesus had not proved to be the Messiah he expected, betrayed the Master to his enemies. After a hasty travesty of a trial, he was condemned by the Sanhedrin as a blasphemer, and the Roman governor was prevailed upon to command his execution. To the dismay of his frightened followers he was crucified. Numb with bewilderment and grief, they could only say, "We trusted that it had been he which should have redeemed Israel." What they had expected we do not know. Perhaps they hardly knew themselves. But they had set all their hopes on Jesus' triumph, and now he had been destroyed by wicked hands.

Destroyed? On the first day of the week following his death it began to be whispered among his followers that he was alive. First one, then another reported having met him. The accounts of the resurrection in the gospels are confusing, and it is impossible to construct from them a clear, consistent story. As to what actually happened to the body of Jesus we may not be able to agree among ourselves. Two facts, however, are certain. The men who had known Jesus most intimately during his life were convinced that he had risen from the dead. And this belief was the inspiration of the whole extraordinary activity of the early church. Though Jesus had been rejected and put to death, his followers were enabled to carry on his work by the assurance that he had been divinely exalted as Lord and Christ and would soon return to usher in the promised Kingdom.

In the endeavor to give definite expression to its faith in Jesus the church has developed many creeds and dogmas about him. The effort was laudable and necessary, but the result has not been altogether fortunate. Not to mention the bitter strife which has often divided Christians into hostile camps of Arians and Athanasians, Monophysites and Dyophysites, Trinitarians and Unitarians, our Christologies have tended to make the person of Jesus vague and unreal. Modern historical study of the gospels has revived interest in the Jesus of history, and we are asking again, "What manner of man is this?" On the foreign-mission field Jesus is being presented as he is in the gospels rather than as he is in the creeds. The impression his personality is making in the Orient is one of the most notable facts of our times. Modern study of the gospels makes all too plain how distressingly little we know about Jesus, but at least it gives us a real person.

It shows us a man of utter sincerity, with a lofty scorn of compromise, willing to make any sacrifice for the right, and demanding the same willingness in his disciples.

"When thine eye is single," he said, "thy whole body also is full of light. . . . No man having put his hand to the plough and looking back is fit for the Kingdom of God. . . . And if thy right eye offend thee, pluck it out and cast it from thee, for it is profitable for thee that one of thy members should perish, and not that thy whole body should be cast into hell. . . . If any man come to me, and hate not his father and mother and wife and children and brethren and sisters, yea, and his own life also, he cannot be my disciple."

With this singleness of purpose went a capacity for blazing indignation. Literature records no more blasting invective than Jesus' denunciations of the cities which rejected his teaching and of the hypocrites among the Pharisees. "Woe unto you, scribes and Pharisees, hypocrites! for ye are like unto whited sepulchres, which indeed appear beautiful outward, but are within full of dead men's bones and of all uncleanness." "Woe unto thee, Chorazin! woe unto thee, Bethsaida! . . . And thou, Capernaum, which art exalted unto heaven, shalt be brought down to hell: for if the mighty works which have been done in thee had been done in Sodom, it would have remained until this day. But I say unto you that it shall be more tolerable for the land of Sodom in the day of judgment than for thee." That the expression of such indignation was not confined to words, let the expulsion of the money-changers from the temple attest.

The natural feelings of humanity are evident again and again in Jesus. We read that he rejoiced, that he sighed, that he was weary, impatient, discouraged. We see him looking to his disciples for understanding, and disap-

pointed when they fail to show it. The feeling most frequently attributed to him, however, is sympathy: "he was
moved with compassion." He understood people; therefore he loved them. When a young man, virtuous but not
satisfied, asked what more he must do, "Jesus beholding
him loved him." When, as he reclined at table, a sinful
woman stood by his couch, bathing his feet with tears and
wiping them off with her hair, he said to his host, who
looked on with disapproval, "Her sins, which are many,
are forgiven, for she loved much." To another woman, in
whose shame self-righteous men had shamelessly exulted,
he said, after sending her accusers away in confusion,
"Hath no man condemned thee? . . . Neither do I condemn thee: go, and sin no more." When his enemies called
him the friend of sinners, they spoke more truly than they
knew.

His sympathy for weakness of the flesh, when the spirit
was willing, did not make him easily imposed upon.
Hypocrisy and guile were transparent to his keen insight,
and he was merciless in condemning them. Again and
again his adversaries endeavored by crafty questions to
inveigle him into some utterance which might be used
against him, but his ready replies, like rapier thrusts, dis-
armed them. It is in this piercing insight into human motives and this quick perception of underlying issues, rather
than in such analytical reasoning as Gautama's, that the
clarity and keenness of Jesus' thinking may be seen. The
same trait is evident in his teaching, which, as we shall see,
insists upon central principles, but leaves details of application to be adjusted to each case and individual. Not subtlety, but crystal-clear simplicity and insight were the dis-

tinctive qualities of his intellect. In thought, as in action, he moved in a straight line.

Perhaps his single-mindedness and simple directness help to explain his love for children. When mothers brought their little ones for him to touch, and the disciples, like officious office-boys, would have sent them away, Jesus said, "Suffer the little children to come unto me, and forbid them not, for of such is the Kingdom of God. Verily I say unto you, whosoever shall not receive the Kingdom of God as a little child, he shall not enter therein." The very childlike qualities which he loved were used by Jesus to rebuke a certain childish egoism in his disciples. Once, when they had been disputing which of them was the greatest, "he took a little child, and set him in the midst of them; and taking him in his arms he said unto them, Whosoever shall receive one of such little children in my name receiveth me, and whosoever shall receive me receiveth not me but him that sent me." That the less lovely traits of children had not escaped his notice is evident when he compares his contemporaries, who would receive neither the asceticism of John the Baptist nor his own more liberal standards, to children playing in the market place and complaining that their fellows would neither dance to their piping nor lament with their mourning.

While Jesus seems to have been interested chiefly in human nature, his sayings evince also a deep appreciation of the beauty shown by field and hillside. The lilies of the field, more gloriously arrayed than Solomon though without toiling or spinning, and the birds of the air, finding their sustenance without anxious sowing and reaping, spoke to him of the Heavenly Father's love for his creatures.

There may be some connection between Jesus' love of Nature and the poetic quality of his sayings. The late Professor C. F. Burney of Oxford has shown that the words of Jesus in the gospels often have the same rhythmic character as the utterances of the prophets in the Old Testament. More important than the verbal form, however, is the essentially poetic nature of the thought. In his inmost spirit Jesus was a poet as well as a prophet. The parable, a favorite form of teaching with him as with the rabbis, gave scope to his imaginative gift for striking comparisons, based always on the simplest experiences of everyday life. A woman putting leaven in three measures of meal or sweeping the house to find a lost coin, a man sowing seed in his field or looking for a lost sheep, the importance of a solid foundation for a house, a father's joy at the return of a wayward son—such were the simple means by which the Galilean teacher conveyed his most profound ideas.

There is a certain playfulness in many of Jesus' sayings. The intensity of his earnestness and the tragedy of his experience did not exclude from his teaching an element of keen though unobtrusive humor. His sense of humor was of that wholesome kind which is the natural outcome of a sense of proportion. It is most characteristically manifested in little word-pictures, lightly sketched with a few masterful strokes, but with a fanciful and amusing exaggeration. For example, meticulous insistence on the smallest details of the Law, while neglecting the fundamental principles on which it rests, is caricatured as anxiously straining out every tiny gnat from one's cup, and then complacently swallowing a whole camel. A rich man's entrance into the Kingdom of God is said to be as impossible as the passage of a camel through the eye of a needle—impossible to man, but not to God. Criticizing others, while unmindful of our own faults, is like offering to pick a speck of dust from another's eye, when there is a beam, a huge piece of lumber, in our own. False humility, on the other hand, is as absurd as covering a lighted candle with a bushel basket.

The same gift of vivid pictorial simile and metaphor, though without such fantastic hyerbole, appears in the charge that the Pharisees wash the outside of the cup and platter but leave the inside dirty. Sometimes the pictures are too terrible to be amusing—the whited sepulchres, the graves over which men walk without knowing that there is death under their feet. Even the most playful of Jesus' figures, indeed, have a deadly earnestness withal. Yet the power of irony which came from his keen sense of the ridiculous was one of his sharpest weapons in the conflict with sham and superficiality.

Another way in which Jesus showed a sense of proportion was his rejection of asceticism. In this he differed markedly from John the Baptist. The enemies of Jesus did not accuse him of fanatical Puritanism, but the very opposite. "John came neither eating nor drinking, and they say, He hath a devil. The Son of Man came eating and drinking, and they say, Behold a gluttonous man and a winebibber, a friend of publicans and sinners!" In line with this attitude was his indifference to the minute restrictions and prescriptions of the traditional Law. The respectable Pharisees noted with horror that he sometimes ate without stopping to wash his hands. The careful definitions of what was permissible and what was forbidden on the Sabbath, which had cost the scribes much thought, he simply ignored. "The Sabbath was made for man," he said, "and not man for the Sabbath."

His independence amazed his hearers. "They were astonished at his teaching, for he taught them as one that had authority, and not as the scribes." It must have taken their breath away to hear him calmly declare, "Ye have heard that it was said by them of old time, . . . but I say unto you—!" If there was ever any doubt or hesitation in his teaching, the records do not show it. He was so sure of the truth of his message that he was ready to die for it and expected his followers to be equally willing to sacrifice themselves. Sometimes the gospels represent him as demanding sacrifice for the sake of the message alone, sometimes as saying also "for my sake." Probably he encouraged personal attachment to himself as a means of securing devotion to the Kingdom.

But there was a limit to his self-assertion. He expressly disclaimed omniscience: "Of that day and that hour knoweth no man, no, not the angels which are in heaven, neither the Son, but the Father." He disclaimed perfect goodness. When a man kneeled before him and addressed him as "Good Master," he said, "Why callest thou me good? There is none good but one, that is God." Accused of healing the sick by the power of the Evil One, he felt that what was serious in the charge was not the insult to himself but the rejection of a work of God's Spirit: "And whosoever speaketh a word against the Son of Man, it shall be forgiven him; but whosoever speaketh against the Holy Spirit, it shall not be forgiven him."

At the heart of all his work and all his teaching was the simple, natural piety of his own soul, his constant sense of intimate communion with his Father. Jesus was no exponent of such mysticism as seeks beatitude in a self-induced trance. To be sure, he may have had occasional moments of intense emotional exaltation, in which he felt the rapture of the mystic's absorbed contemplation. A few incidents in the gospels—the vision of the Spirit at Jesus' baptism, the transfiguration, the experience reflected in the exultant saying, "I beheld Satan as lightning fall from heaven"—may be so interpreted. But there is a tendency on the part of many writers at present to find such phenomena everywhere, and the evidence for them in the life of Jesus is at most ambiguous. The gospels have no such stories as those of Mahavira's insensibility to his surroundings when absorbed in meditation. Even when Jesus withdrew from the crowds and sought solitude, he was keenly aware of the needs and sorrows of the human beings about him.

If by mysticism is meant, however, not rapt absorption but the daily and hourly "practice of the presence of God," then Jesus was certainly a mystic. His religious experience was characterized by a steady, quiet, uninterrupted sense of oneness with his heavenly Father. We read of his praying on a mountainside by night, or rising early in the morning for prayer. He was a Jew, not a Hindu, and his chief aspiration was not to lose his individuality in contemplating Absolute Reality, but to do the will of the Father who sent him.

His complete consecration to the divine will explains the singleness of purpose and the indifference to either legal or metaphysical subtlety which we have already marked as characteristic of Jesus. It also accounts for another quality which was especially evident as the close of his life drew near, his quiet but unshakable courage. To see rejection and failure like an impenetrable wall before his face, and to realize that after only a brief attempt to make the nation ready for God's Kingdom he must go down to a bitter and shameful death in the very flower of early manhood, was enough to make the stoutest heart quail. That Jesus felt it deeply is evident in his agonizing cry, "O my Father, if it be possible, let this cup pass from me." Yet "he steadfastly set his face to go to Jerusalem," and to the petition just quoted he added, "Nevertheless not as I will, but as Thou wilt." There must be some truth in the statement of the fourth gospel, that when his enemies, coming upon him in the garden, said they were seeking Jesus of Nazareth, and he replied, "I am he," the calm majesty of his bearing so amazed them that "they went backward and fell to the ground."

The teaching of Jesus, like his religious experience, was of a distinctly Jewish type. He inherited the ideas and ideals of the Old Testament. For all his independence of the traditions of the scribes, he was loyal to the Law in its primary intent; in fact the sum of his complaint against the scribes was, "Thus have ye made the commandment of God of none effect by your tradition." When asked what was the first and greatest of all the commandments, he replied with the opening verse of the *Shema,* the quotation from Deuteronomy which is to this day the real creed of Judaism, taught to children at an early age and repeated daily on rising and retiring: "Hear, O Israel; the Lord our God is one Lord; and thou shalt love the Lord thy God with all thy heart, and with all thy soul, and with all thy might."

In like manner all the terms in which his teaching was presented and the ideas which he expressed were Jewish through and through. His most characteristic sayings are closely paralleled in the sayings of the rabbis. No single item in his teaching, in fact, was really new to his hearers. The only difference between his position and that of other Jewish teachers was one of emphasis and proportion, and even here there were those among the Jews who could say to him, "Well, Master, thou hast said the truth," and to whom he could say, "Thou art not far from the Kingdom of God." That he even regarded himself as having a mission for the Jews alone is explicitly stated in the New Testament: "I am not sent but unto the lost sheep of the house of Israel." The bearing of these facts on the real originality and universality of Jesus' teaching may be discussed after we have briefly considered what that teaching is.

It all revolves about the conception of God as being Lord of heaven and earth, and at the same time the loving Father who numbers the very hairs of our heads. This was not a new idea of God, but it gained new meaning and importance from the place it held in Jesus' own experience. Both phases of the conception—God's universal sovereignty and his loving purpose for his children—find expression in the doctrine of the Kingdom. To Jesus, as to his contemporaries, the Kingdom of God meant both God's present dominion over all his creation and the future reign of God which would follow the succession of human empires. In this future Kingdom the will of God would be completely realized, and his power and authority would prevail over all the powers of evil. While this involved the judgment of the wicked, Jesus did not, like John, stress "the wrath to come" but emphasized rather the joys of the Father's Kingdom. His message was a gospel, *i.e., good news.*

How far Jesus shared the apocalyptic expectations which were current among the Jews in his day is disputed by scholars. It is certain, however, that he did not mean by the coming of the Kingdom the gradual establishment of social justice in the earth. The Kingdom which he proclaimed was to be a divine Kingdom, divinely established. Its coming presupposed the resurrection of the dead and the judgment. Its power might be felt in advance through such signs as the healing of the sick, and those who were prepared for it might be said to be already in the Kingdom or to have the Kingdom within (or among) them, but the full consummation lay in the future, when the dead would be raised and the present order would come to an end.

Just how Jesus thought of his own relation to the Kingdom of God is uncertain. He seems to have accepted the apocalyptic doctrine that the Kingdom would be ushered in by the Son of Man, who would come on the clouds of heaven and judge the earth; also the gospels represent him as applying the term "Son of Man" to himself. Many New Testament scholars, however, are convinced that this identification was made by the early church, and that Jesus did not consider himself the heavenly Son of Man. In the same way the title of Messiah was applied to Jesus by his early followers. In its Greek form, Christ, it became his most common appellation. Yet it is by no means certain that he considered himself the Messiah. Again, many passages in the gospels indicate that he regarded himself, not only as one of God's children, but as the Son of God in a unique sense. In connection with his baptism and at the transfiguration a quotation from the second Psalm is given: "Thou art my beloved Son." This was doubtless understood by the early Christians to mean, "Thou art the Messiah." Whether that was what it meant to Jesus himself, or, if not, what it did mean, we cannot be sure. Recent investigators tend to believe that Jesus thought of his mission simply as that of a prophet. In that case all these other designations were applied to him by his followers in the attempt to express their sense of his supreme significance.

One other interpretation of his work must be noted in this connection. The first Christians saw in their Master the fulfilment of the prophetic poems on the Servant of the Lord in the latter part of the book of Isaiah. The fifty-third chapter of Isaiah particularly seemed to be an exact representation of the character, the tragic fate, and the saving sacrifice of Jesus. Here again New Testament scholars are inclined to believe that it was the church rather than Jesus himself who first put this interpretation upon his mission, but in this case there is less reason to doubt that Jesus so understood his own work, at least toward the end of his life when his rejection by the nation as a whole had become evident. It is not at all improbable that when he read, "He is despised and rejected of men, a man of sorrows and acquainted with grief," and, "Surely he hath borne our griefs and carried our sorrows," he saw his own life's story foreshadowed and its meaning made clear. One gospel tells us that he described his work as the fulfilment of another passage from the same book: "The Spirit of the Lord is upon me, because he hath anointed me to preach the gospel to the poor." It is noteworthy that the word "anointed" is connected in this passage with preaching good news to the poor, for, as we have seen, the Messiah is the Anointed One.

With regard to the conditions of entrance into the Kingdom there is no uncertainty. Repentance and faith (that is, believing the good news and trusting God for the establishment of the Kingdom) were the requirements which Jesus held before his hearers. Repentance, of course, involved a life of obedience to the will of God, and this meant a life of utter consecration, no matter what sacrifice it might necessitate. The Kingdom was worth any sacrifice, Jesus said; it was like a precious pearl, or a treasure found in a field, for which a man would sell all that he had. The will of God was expressed in the Law, but we have already noted that Jesus interpreted the Law according to inner principles and rejected the traditions of the scribes. In this he championed the simple piety of the "people of the land," to whom he belonged, as against the meticulous legalism of the Pharisees. True obedience to the Law was not the outer observance of precepts but the inward righteousness of the spirit. This required not less but more than the righteousness of the scribes and Pharisees. The sum and substance of it all was love for God and for one's neighbor. To be a true child of God one must love all men impartially and disinterestedly, just as the heavenly Father "maketh his sun to rise on the evil and on the good, and sendeth rain on the just and on the unjust." A practical measure of such love is the principle of doing to others as we should like them to do to us.

The consistent application of the principles of Jesus' teaching would result in social justice, but Jesus was not a social reformer. He did not condemn war or slavery, so far as the records indicate. Wealth he viewed with distrust as destructive of the spiritual life; naturally, therefore, he ignored the economic basis of civilization as well as the institutions of society. Only in the case of marriage is anything approaching definite legislation attributed to him. Though unmarried himself, and though convinced that some must abjure marriage for the sake of the Kingdom, he taught that monogamous marriage was sacred and permanent. Divorce and remarriage he denounced as adultery. Respect for one's parents also he exalted as a sacred obligation, in spite of the fact that loyalty to the Kingdom might occasionally require forsaking parents, wives, children, brothers, and sisters alike. The payment of the taxes demanded by the hated Roman oppressors was at least tacitly allowed by the saying, "Render unto Cæsar the things that are Cæsar's," but Jesus was much more concerned that his followers should render "unto God the things that are God's." To a man who requested his intervention in a quarrel over the division of an estate Jesus said, "Man, who made me a judge or a divider over you?" Not the reform of social institutions but the production of right attitudes in individuals was his primary objective.

At the same time it must not be forgotten that his conception of the will of God, by obedience to which one gained entrance to the Kingdom, was distinctly ethical, not ritualistic. Love for God, the first requirement, carried with it love for men as its necessary corollary. "Therefore if thou bring thy gift to the altar, and there remember that thy

brother hath aught against thee, leave there thy gift before
the altar and go thy way; first be reconciled to thy brother,
and then come and offer thy gift." "And when ye stand
praying, forgive, if ye have aught against any one; that
your Father also which is in heaven may forgive you your
trespasses."

The question of Jesus' originality has been raised by the
discovery that every item in his teaching may be duplicated
in Jewish writings. It becomes still more pressing when we
recall that even in far-off China, many centuries before
Jesus' day, Confucius had formulated the Golden Rule,
and Lao-tze had declared that one should return good for
evil. Without attempting an exhaustive discussion of the
matter, we may here remark that truth is much more important in a religious doctrine than novelty. The fact that
a principle has been enunciated before does not make it
less true or less important. The true religion must include
what is true in all religions. Furthermore a new emphasis
may be given without the addition of new details, and
Jesus' emphasis on inner spirituality as against outer correctness was needed. To these considerations we must add
that Jesus gave a fresh and beautiful expression to the old
ideas; also he embodied them in his own life and character:
in him the word was made flesh.

The universality as well as the originality of his teaching may be questioned when one realizes how thoroughly
Jewish he was. Here we need only observe that the real
question is not in what terms his teaching was delivered
or to what audience, but whether it is universally applica-
ble and true. There is nothing essentially exclusive or of
limited application in Jesus' teaching. If what he said is

true at all, it is true for all men. Jewish in origin and in form, it is concerned with nothing but what is common to man, and it sets no conditions of salvation which may not be met by the Gentile as well as by the Jew. If in its spread among the Gentiles Christianity assimilated many ideas and practices quite alien to the teaching of Jesus, it was not because anything that he taught had to be omitted or altered to make the religion tenable by Gentiles. Indeed the church to-day is coming more and more to see that Christianity can be truly universal only in so far as it can clear away the growths of many years and get back to Jesus.

CHAPTER ELEVEN

CONCLUSION

THE purpose of this little book is not to discuss or to interpret, but simply to present the stories of the founders of the world's religions. That purpose, strictly speaking, calls for no conclusion. The reader may be left to draw conclusions for himself. By way of summary, however, it may be of some advantage to attempt a brief comparison of the most important doctrines and ideals of these great teachers.

The task is a somewhat delicate one. In no field are comparisons more odious than in religion. It must be distinctly understood that we are not concerned to demonstrate the superiority of one founder over the others. In the first place, such a purpose would make a fair comparison impossible. Furthermore, judgments of superiority and inferiority imply a standard of evaluation, and this standard determines the result as much as do the facts compared. If, for instance, we compare the civilization of Europe and Asia on the basis of European ideas and tastes, naturally we shall find European civilization superior. So also one who estimates the relative values of different religions, assuming all the while the standards of his own religion, will automatically arrive at the conclusion that his own religion is the best.

And, after all, why should we jealously set one faith over against another in opposition? Of course religions and their founders are not actually on an even plane of excellence. One, undoubtedly, is truer and greater than the rest, and we should have our own convictions as to which is the best. But it is more important to appreciate them all than to be able to write a Q.E.D. after our own confession of faith. At any rate, we cannot judge between the faiths and their founders until we know just what they have in common and wherein they differ.

It is not easy, at first sight, to discern any unity at all in these religions of different lands and times. One fundamental assumption, however, seems to underlie all of them. Not one of our founders regards the world as governed by chance, or by merely physical forces. Be it the will of a personal Deity or the operation of an impersonal principle, some spiritual power regulates the destinies of men. Furthermore, this power is moral in its working, for the universe is so governed that right-doing is rewarded and wrong-doing is punished. That the moral values of human life have their basis and their sanctions only within the social group is quite alien to the thought of any of these teachers. Even Confucius holds that Heaven has implanted a good nature in man, and that the moral order is grounded in the nature of the universe. In spite of all the great differences in the forms which this conviction takes—or perhaps just because of the differences—the importance of this basic agreement can hardly be exaggerated.

The differences must not be ignored, however. They are as real and as important as the agreement. With regard to the nature of the power governing the universe there is the greatest variety of belief among the founders. Lao-tze, adoring the Tao, and Confucius, relying upon Heaven, are both apparently agnostic, or at least non-committal, regarding a personal Heavenly Emperor. Mahavira and Buddha reject both personal theism and abstract monism, retaining only Karma as controlling human destiny. Gautama, it is true, seems to have admitted the existence of the popular gods, but he did not ascribe to them the power to govern life and nature.

All the other founders believe in a personal God. No founder teaches polytheism. The polytheistic religions of the earth have not had individual founders. Moses, to be sure, was not strictly a monotheist: probably he did not question the reality of the gods of other peoples. He did insist, however, on the exclusive worship of Jehovah by the Hebrews. Genuine monotheism was taught by Zoroaster, Jesus, and Mohammed, while in Nanak we find a mixture of Hindu monism and Moslem monotheism. Here, as elsewhere, the influence of inherited conceptions is evident. Each founder, whether he adopts or rejects the prevailing views of his day, remains distinctly and characteristically Chinese, Indian, Iranian, or Semitic, as the case may be.

With monotheism goes omnipotence. Mohammed, followed to a considerable degree by Nanak, lays more stress upon this attribute of God than Jesus and Zoroaster do, though both of these also look for the complete and final triumph of God's kingdom and regard Him as the Maker and Ruler of all. Not even Mohammed denies that there are evil powers at war with God, but their power is limited and their ultimate downfall certain. With Mohammed and Nanak predestination, a corollary of strict monotheism, is made explicit and emphatic, though every man is held responsible for his acts. Moses, in regarding Yahweh as the mightiest of all gods, approaches the idea of omnipotence.

How far mercy and love are predicated of God by the founders is sometimes hard to say. In later Judaism God is "merciful and gracious, long-suffering and abundant in goodness." His deliverance of the Hebrews from Egyptian bondage is regarded as a manifestation of compassion, and there seems to be no reason to doubt that Moses himself so thought of it. Mohammed constantly spoke of Allah as "the Compassionate, the Merciful." Both Moses and Mohammed, however, laid more stress upon the righteous wrath of God than on His loving kindness. Even less prominent is the attribute of love in Zoroaster's teaching. Nanak is more inclined to emphasize it, but of all the founders Jesus is the only one who exalts God's love as basic and universal. Of course such a quality could hardly be attributed to the impersonal powers or principles recognized in the religions of India and China, though some forms of all these religions have found room for beliefs in friendly deities.

With regard to the hereafter we find again a great diversity of ideas, together with a certain underlying agreement, though in this case the agreement is not unanimous, except in the fact that some form of existence after death is recognized. Lao-tze and Moses, far apart as they were in the positive aspects of their teaching, were alike in having nothing to say about the life to come. Moses, doubtless, shared the primitive belief in an underworld (Sheol), and Lao-tze tacitly admitted the existence of ancestral spirits. Neither the Hebrew legislator nor the Chinese philosopher, however, held out any hope of blessedness after death. Nor did Confucius, for while insisting on due reverence for the dead and a conscientious performance of the rites of ancestor-worship, he seems to have had in mind the effect on the living rather than the needs or pleasures of the

departed. He also discouraged inquiry about the other
world by saying, "When you do not know life, why ask
about death?" So far as we can see, none of these three
teachers drew any distinction between the lot of the righteous and that of the wicked after death.

The other six (that is, two-thirds of the total number) all
teach some kind of retribution beyond the grave. Mahavira,
Gautama, and Nanak retain the ancient belief in Karma,
working through many successive reincarnations. In addition to this Nanak speaks also of hell as the abode of the
wicked, and Jainism recognizes many hells and purgatories
as way-stations between different incarnations. Of course
the retributive effects of Karma are inherent and auto-
matic, more like the operations of a natural law than the
rewards or penalties decreed by a judge. Salvation means
to these three teachers of India, as to the Brahman philosophers before them, deliverance from the endless round
of birth and death. Mahavira probably thought of the state
of the delivered as one of conscious or super-conscious bliss.
How Gautama conceived it we cannot tell: since there
was no soul, Nirvana could not be the extinction of the
soul, but it was at least the extinction of suffering and of
the desire which causes suffering. For Nanak the ultimate
goal was complete absorption into Brahma. Far different is
the conception of the future life in the religions of western
Asia. Instead of transmigration and release from transmigration, Zoroaster spoke of resurrection, judgment, and
either Paradise or Hell. In Judaism also these beliefs developed, probably through Zoroastrian influence, but not
until long after the time of Moses. Jesus retained them as a

part of his Jewish inheritance, and through Judaism and Christianity they passed into Islam.

With such diverse conceptions of the goal, the founders naturally differ on the ways by which salvation is achieved. They are not agreed as to the need of a Deliverer. Reliance on one's own unaided efforts is required by Gautama and Mahavira. "Man!" says the latter, "Thou art thy own friend! Why wishest thou for a friend beyond thyself?" Lao-tze and Confucius also seem to feel no need of spiritual resources beyond the individual's own will-power. For the Chinese and the Indian founders alike, however, the attainment of the end in view depends in some sense on conformity to the nature of things. Man cannot devise his own way of salvation. He must live in harmony with the Tao, in obedience to the laws of Heaven, or in accordance with the principle of Karma.

In the theistic religions he is dependent not upon a law or principle but upon the will of God. With Mohammed and Nanak this dependence is so magnified that little room is left for the individual's part in his own deliverance. At the same time men are judged according to their deeds, as in Zoroastrianism and Christianity. Moses too believed that Yahweh punished and rewarded his people as they kept or disobeyed his laws, but the rewards and punishments were of a purely temporal nature and were visited upon the people as a whole.

In every religion, whether man is wholly or only partly left to work out his salvation for himself, he must meet certain requirements. What these are is a matter of much difference of opinion among the founders of the faiths, but on one point they agree. All of them demand a righteous life. Not one teaches a merely ritualistic or a purely mystical way of salvation. All too frequently adherents of all these faiths have put their trust in ritual acts or mystical experiences as all-sufficient, but they have thereby fallen short of the ideals of their masters. In the relative degree of importance attached to ethical requirements, and still more in their ideas of what constitutes right living, the founders differ widely. That they all, however, make good conduct at least one step in the way of life is a fact of great significance.

No founder makes morality the sole condition of salvation. Sometimes, even when conduct is of primary importance, certain ritual observances also are essential. In the case of Confucius, perhaps, it would be more accurate to say that the ceremonies are a means of moral education than that they are acts by which one gains salvation. The fact remains, however, that they are an integral element in his teaching. The ritualistic emphasis is very strong in Zoroastrianism. How far this was true of the original teaching of the prophet we do not know, but prayers and offerings with the sacred fire, at least, were presupposed if not commanded. Mohammed ordered fasting, pilgrimages, and stated prayers as well as charity and righteous living. Moses made no distinction between ritual and moral laws. Ceremonial requirements are not prominent in the teaching of Nanak, but some merit is ascribed to the performance of the rites. The doctrine of dependence on the Guru, who conveys the saving grace of God by uttering a sacred formula, is decidedly ritualistic, but the ritualistic element in it may have developed after Nanak's death. No ceremonies were prescribed by Lao-tze, Mahavira, or Gautama.

Jesus seems to have accepted and observed the rites of his ancestral faith. He also accepted baptism at the hands of John, and he probably sanctioned its practice by his followers. That he intended at the Last Supper to institute a sacramental rite is very doubtful. Certainly he laid no stress on ceremonies.

Mystical experience, though not necessarily of the ecstatic kind, is more highly regarded than ritual by these founders of religions. Most of the founders were mystics themselves. Naturally, therefore, they valued the experience of mystical union as a means of salvation, if not as the end itself. Lao-tze prized it highly, though a quiet life of inner harmony is more prominent in his teaching than occasional blissful ecstasies. Of course for Lao-tze mystical experience did not mean communion with a personal deity, but something like the Stoic's joy in being "in tune with the Infinite." A pantheistic conception of union with the Absolute was held by Nanak also, who, following the ancient sages of his native land, regarded ultimate absorption in the All as the essential meaning of salvation. Mahavira rejected the monistic philosophy of the Brahmans; consequently he did not use the idea of reabsorption into Brahma. Mystical beatitude, indeed, is not especially prominent in his recorded teaching. Nevertheless the stories told of his utter obliviousness to his surroundings while lost in meditation indicate that such experiences were highly prized by him and by his followers. With Gautama the ethical requirements of religion took first place, yet it must not be forgotten that the final step in the Eightfold Path is mystical absorption.

Like the teachers of India and China, with the notable exception of Confucius, those of Western Asia also were all apparently more or less given to visions. They did not in their teaching, however, emphasize such experiences as necessary for salvation nor offer a technique for cultivating them. Zoroaster, Mohammed, and Nanak received their revelations through visions. Moses' vision of the burning bush and Jesus' experience of the descent of the Holy Spirit at his baptism probably were of a more or less ecstatic character. But by this very fact these prophets were distinctly set apart from their followers. What the people had to do was simply to accept and obey the revelation of the prophet. Jesus differed from the others in that he expected his disciples to experience an intimate communion with the Father like his own. Thus he made a kind of mysticism an essential part of the way of salvation—not, to be sure, the type of mysticism cherished in India, but the quiet, habitual practice of personal prayer.

Correct belief has often been emphasized as necessary for salvation, but the founders of the faiths lay relatively little stress upon it. To some extent, of course, it is assumed by all of them. Sometimes also it is explicitly demanded. Mohammed was perhaps the one who attached most importance to it. Jesus had much to say about faith, but what he meant was an attitude of trust and confidence rather than the acceptance of particular doctrines. Right belief is one of the Three Jewels of Jainism and one of the steps in Buddha's Eightfold Path. In no case, however, does it seem to be of equal weight with righteous conduct.

In their beliefs regarding God and the hereafter, in their conceptions of the meaning of salvation, and in their views of what is necessary to attain salvation, the founders occupy, as we have seen, a great variety of positions. The same diversity is evident in their ethical ideals. They differ not only in the relative importance they ascribe to conduct but also in their ideas as to what right living means. Of course they are unanimous on some points. What may be called the fundamental virtues are taught by all of them. No founder, for example, encourages selfishness, cowardice, or dishonesty. Truthfulness is especially exalted by Zoroaster and Nanak, and Mahavira's followers are noted for their honesty in business. Sensual indulgence has sometimes been encouraged by religion, but not by any of the founders of the great faiths of mankind.

All of them, moreover, agree that "a man's life consisteth not in the abundance of the things which he possesseth." Lao-tze recommended what we call "the simple life," and Jesus said that men should be as free as the birds and flowers from concern for food and clothing. Both Jesus and Confucius used the figure of becoming like little children. In praising simplicity and humility, indeed, the two great Chinese sages and the Galilean Jew agreed. On the other hand, they did not teach asceticism. Lao-tze's quiet and unstriving life was not one of self-torture. Jesus "came eating and drinking," and his followers were criticized for not fasting like the followers of John the Baptist. Confucius, though he said that poverty should be preferred to wealth unjustly gained, attached no little value to material prosperity. So did Zoroaster. Mohammed, in the earlier part of his career, practised austerities, but, except for the observance of a month of fasting every year, he did not discourage worldly goods and pleasures. Nanak too was an ascetic for a while but later definitely renounced that way of life. The most extreme contempt for all the good things of this life was shown by Gautama and Mahavira, and even Gautama was not the radical ascetic that Mahavira was. Indeed the Buddha, after his Enlightenment, abandoned self-mortification, yet his Middle Way remains a way of world-denial. In spite of these divergent points of view, good character and conduct were worth far more in the eyes of all these spiritual guides than all the treasures of the world.

Perhaps the most far-reaching difference between the founders is in their attitudes toward normal social relationships. With regard to marriage in particular they agree only in demanding marital fidelity. Zoroaster, Moses, and Mohammed allowed and practised polygamy and provided for divorce. The position of woman is distinctly lower than that of man with all the founders except Jesus. He alone— the only one of them who was not or had not been married—gave a clear ideal of marriage as a binding, permanent union of one man and one woman on an equal footing. He was more concerned, it is true, with individual righteousness and with the future Kingdom of God than with any social institution, and he held the most precious social bonds subordinate to the Kingdom. Nevertheless he insisted on the sacredness of marriage and of filial obligations. In Buddhism and Jainism celibacy is required of the monks. Indeed these two religions, having monasticism as their central feature, are essentially un-social, if not anti-social. They have their lay adherents, to be sure, and hold for them substantially the same ideals as other religions. Only the monk, however, can attain deliverance. Nanak, while much inclined to separate himself from normal ties, did not require monastic seclusion as the way of salvation.

Neither did Lao-tze teach withdrawal from society, in spite of his unworldly ideal of life. Confucius, Zoroaster, Moses, and Mohammed were actively interested in social welfare.

A similar variety of attitudes toward government may be observed. Lao-tze had much to say on the subject although his conception of good government was peculiar. The people, he declared, should be kept in ignorance, and the rulers should set a good example by doing nothing. Confucius too believed that kings should rule by good example rather than by force, but he also favored active and positive political measures. Good government, he said, required sufficient food, sufficient military equipment, and the confidence of the people, and the greatest of these was the confidence of the people. Confucius was himself a practical and successful administrator. Moses and Mohammed were both legislators and executives. The value of good government was stressed by Zoroaster also, but Mahavira, Buddha, and Nanak seem to have had little interest in affairs of state, except as rulers helped or hindered in the propagation of their teachings. The nearest thing to a political pronouncement in the teaching of Jesus is the cryptic saying, "Render therefore unto Cæsar the things which are Cæsar's, and unto God the things which are God's."

In view of present-day movements to abolish war, and particularly to advance the cause of peace through religious agencies, it is interesting to note the teaching of the founders on this subject. Moses worshipped "Yahweh of Armies," who fought with Israel on the field of battle. Zoroaster and Mohammed regarded war as laudable and useful for the propagation of the truth. The ideal of Confucius was a peaceful one, exalting the scholar above the soldier, but he did not deprecate the use of force when circumstances seemed to demand it. In the teaching of Lao-tze, on the other hand, war is plainly and emphatically denounced. Gautama also condemned it, though with reservations. Nanak was pained by the suffering of the people in a time of invasion, but neither he nor Mahavira seems to have left any definite declaration on the moral significance of war. Jesus also had nothing to say about it, unless it be the saying, "They that take the sword shall perish with the sword." The Christian attitude toward war, as toward slavery and other evils, is a matter of the implications of disinterested love.

Our founders disagree not only on particular ethical questions but even on underlying principles. Their conceptions of the essential nature of the righteous life are different. With Gautama and Mahavira the great aim is to escape from Karma by abolishing desire. Lao-tze's doctrine of inactivity is based on imitation of the Way of Nature. The *summum bonum* for Confucius is the stability and welfare of the body politic. Active participation on the right side of the cosmic struggle is the basic principle of Zoroaster's teaching. Laws revealed from heaven are taught by Moses and Mohammed; hence faithfulness to the covenant with the former and submissive obedience with the latter are the governing conceptions. Jesus also defines righteousness in terms of obedience to the Law, but under the controlling principle of love for God and man. As a practical formula for the expression of this love the Golden Rule is given. Confucius gives essentially the same formula. His application of it, however, is determined by the standard of reciprocity rather than by love. Lao-tze and Nanak alone agree with Jesus in the ideal of returning good for evil. No single, dominating principle is evident in Nanak's ethical teaching.

Through all this confusing variety of ideals and conceptions there are a few points which stand out as of primary importance. Is the Power which rules our lives a Person or a blind, inexorable law or principle? If a Person, is He an arbitrary Sovereign or a loving Father? Is the ultimate goal of human life extinction and release from suffering, is it absorption into the Source of Being, or is it a continued or renewed existence of a positive and joyous kind and in a better world than this? Is the true ideal of life one of negation and withdrawal from the contacts and pursuits of human society, or is it one of active participation, of enjoyment, and of effort for improvement in the world? Is reality to be found in the normal, conscious experiences which we share with one another, or in closing the gates of sense, detaching ourselves from ordinary consciousness, and entering into a different, extraordinary kind of experience? On such questions as these we must frankly recognize the differences between the faiths of men. Here we must make our choice, each person for himself. But having done so, when we find ourselves at variance with this or that great spiritual leader, we can still acknowledge gladly the world's debt to him and his importance for the spiritual progress of mankind.

Furthermore, the variety of their creeds and points of view makes all the more significant the things the founders held in common. Few as these are, they are of the utmost importance. In the recognition of some ruling power in the universe, and in the faith that it is on the side of righteousness, the personally founded religions are at one. Here followers of all these teachers have ground for mutual respect and sympathy. Their unanimity in these basic convictions also brings renewed assurance and in some degree confirms our common faith.

SUGGESTIONS FOR FURTHER READING

This bibliography is selective, not comprehensive. Its purpose is to recommend, not the latest or even the most authoritative books, but (A) one or two good books in English to read *first* regarding each founder; (B) two books which present the lives of the founders (or some of them) from points of view other than that of the present book; and (C) some standard reference works where further material and more complete bibliographies may be found.

(A)

Lao-tze: Carus, P. *The Canon of Reason and Virtue.* (Open Court, 1913.) Text and translation of the Tao-Teh-King.

Confucius: Legge, J. *Confucius, His Life and Teachings.* (Lippincott, 1875.)

Lao-tze and Confucius: Soothill, W. E. *The Three Religions of China.* (Oxford, 1913.)

—— Legge, J. *The Religions of China.* (Hodder & Stoughton, London, and Scribners, New York, 1880.)

Mahavira: Stevenson, M. *The Heart of Jainism.* (Oxford, 1915.)

Buddha: Carus, P. *The Gospel of Buddha.* (Open Court, 1912.) Translation of selections from the Buddhist scriptures.

—— Saunders, K. J. *Gotama Buddha, a Biography.* (Association Press, 1920.) Based directly on some of the Buddhist scriptures.

Zoroaster: Jackson, A. V. W. *Zoroaster, the Prophet of Ancient Iran.* (Macmillan, 1901.) An important scholarly study.

Moses: Fleg, E. *The Life of Moses.* (Gollancz, London, and Dutton, New York, 1928.) An English translation of a brilliant French book portraying Moses as he appears in the legends of the Rabbis.

Mohammed: Ali, Ameer Syed. *The Spirit of Islam.* (Christopher, London, and Doran, New York, 1923.) A life of the prophet by a liberal Moslem scholar.

Mohammed: Rodwell, J. M. *The Koran.* (Dent, Everyman's Library, London, and Dutton, New York, 1909.) One of the standard English translations, arranged in what is believed to be chronological order.

Nanak: Macauliffe, M. A. *The Sikh Religion: Its Gurus, Sacred Writings and Authors.* (6 vols.) Vol. I. (Oxford, 1909.)

Jesus: Bosworth, E. I. *The Life and Teachings of Jesus According to the First Three Gospels.* (Macmillan, 1924.)

(B)

Van Buskirk, W. R. *The Saviors of Mankind.* (Macmillan, 1929.) An interpretation of the lives and teachings of the founders and other religious leaders in relation to their social environments. Valuable in spite of a tendency to draw on imagination where facts are not available.

Beck, L. A. *The Story of Oriental Philosophy.* (Cosmopolitan Book Corp., London and New York, 1928.) Interesting chapters on some of the founders by a talented writer who has studied Oriental life and thought at first hand. More appreciative than critical.

(C)

Moore, G. F. *History of Religions.* 2 vols. (Scribners, 1913–1919.) By all odds the best general history of religions in English. Good bibliography.

Hastings, J. (editor). *Encyclopedia of Religion and Ethics.* 12 vols. (Scribner's, 1908–1922.) Articles by competent authorities, with exhaustive index.

Müller, F. M. (editor). *Sacred Books of the East.* 50 vols. (Oxford, 1879–1910.) Scriptures of most of the religions in English translation, with exhaustive index.

INDEX

Ahimsa, 73.
Ahura Mazda, 115 f.
Allah, 163.
Amesha Spentas, 117.
Ancestry of Confucius, 33.
 Mahavira, 64.
 Buddha, 78.
 Mohammed, 150.
 Nanak, 173.
 Jesus, 196.
Apocalyptic hope, 199, 217.
Archangels, 117.
Asceticism, 63, 67 f., 75 f., 83, 179
 f., 192, 212, 232.
Atman, 61 f.
Authorship, *see Literary Activity.*

Baptism of Jesus, 203.
Birth of Lao-tze, 12.
 Confucius, 33.
 Mahavira, 64.
 Buddha, 78.
 Zoroaster, 106 f.
 Moses, 125.
 Mohammed, 151.
 Nanak, 173.
 Jesus, 196.
Books written by the Founders, *see
 Literary Activity.*
Brahman, 61 f.
Brahmanism, 59 ff., 170 f.

Caste, 59, 76, 170, 192.
Character of Lao-tze, 22 f.
 Confucius, 43 ff.
 Mahavira, 77.
 Buddha, 79 ff., 93 f.
 Zoroaster, 110 f., 115.
 Moses, 146.
 Mohammed, 153 f., 160 f.
 Nanak, 185 f.
 Jesus, 207 ff.

Childhood of Lao-tze, 13.
 Confucius, 33.
 Mahavira, 67.
 Buddha, 79.
 Zoroaster, 108 f.
 Moses, 126.
 Mohammed, 152.
 Nanak, 173 ff.
 Jesus, 196 f.
Climate, Influence of, 105.
Covenant, 138 f., 149.

Death of Lao-tze, 16.
 Confucius, 39.
 Mahavira, 69.
 Buddha, 92 f.
 Zoroaster, 114.
 Moses, 148.
 Mohammed, 160.
 Nanak, 185.
 Jesus, 206.
Drink, Sacred, *see Haoma.*
Dualism (Metaphysical), 62 f., 70
 f., 94.
Dualism (Theological and Practical), 106, 117 f.

Eightfold Path, 100 f.
Enlightenment of Buddha, 84.
Ethical Teaching of Lao-tze, 24 ff.
 Confucius, 54 ff.
 Mahavira, 72 ff.
 Buddha, 97 ff.
 Zoroaster, 122 f.
 Moses, 140 f., 149.
 Mohammed, 161 f., 168.
 Nanak, 191 f.
 Jesus, 220 f.
 Comparison, 228 f., 232 f.
Experience, Religious, of Lao-tze,
 22 f.
 Confucius, 49.